D0261063

101 GINS

TO TRY BEFORE YOU DIE

101 GINS

TO TRY BEFORE YOU DIE

IAN BUXTON

BIRLINN

This edition first published in 2018
by Birlinn Ltd
West Newington House
10 Newington Road
Edinburgh EH9 1QS

www.birlinn.co.uk

Copyright © Ian Buxton, 2015, 2018
First edition published in 2015

ISBN 978 1 78027 565 9

1

All rights reserved. No part of this publication may be reproduced, stored,
or transmitted in any form, or by any means electronic, mechanical or
photocopying, recording or otherwise, without the express written
permission of the publisher.

The moral right of Ian Buxton to be identified as the author of this work
has been asserted by him in accordance with the Copyright, Designs and
Patents Act 1988

British Library Cataloguing-in-Publication Data
A catalogue record for this book is available on request from
the British Library

Designed by Teresa Monachino
Printed and bound by PNB Print, Latvia

CONTENTS

INTRODUCTION

We're in the middle of a new Gin Craze. From being the drink of choice of middle-aged, Jaguar-driving golfers and an easy target for stand-up comedians, today it's harder to find anything hipper on the international bar scene.

This is by way of an exploration. I want to see how Madam Geneva, scourge of the drinking classes and emblematic of wantonness, sin and ruin, has evolved into the most fashionable of spirits. How a drink reeking of suburbia, Home Counties complacency and golf-club lounges is now found in cutting-edge cocktail bars around the world. And how what you might once have described as the Nigel Farage of drinks has morphed into its Cara Delevingne. (*Disclaimer:* I have no idea what the divine Cara drinks. We move in different circles, and for all I know she's tucked up in bed well before *News at Ten* with a tasty glass of organic green tea – the point, as I'm sure you've gathered, is that gin is *hot.*)[1]

Rowlandson and, famously, Hogarth placed gin at the heart of much of their work. Commentators too, such as Defoe, Fielding, Dickens and many others, had much to say about it, not to mention those eighteenth-century politicians who legislated with such enthusiasm (and such a lack of noticeable effect) to curb the English taste for gin.

Or should that be Dutch? They gave the world 'genever' which the English made their own, leading rapidly to London's original (and infamous) Gin Craze. It may have taken more than 250 years, but gin has now shaken off its reputation for debauchery and ruin to take its place as one of the hottest of world spirits.

So, from Adnams to Xoriguer (couldn't find a Z I liked; you'll see) and London to Plymouth (and beyond) I want to explore this incredible explosion of innovative gin brands and the new generation of young and enthusiastic distillers that are reinventing this most English of drinks.

Not that a hint of debauchery and ruin does its image any harm. But today it's all very confusing. Scarcely a day goes by without an

---

[1] Though conventionally served ice cold, of course.

established brand offering a fresh take on their established styles or, more likely, a new boutique distillery opening its doors – where gin is *de rigueur*. However, before we dive into that particular madness a little bit of history is probably called for.

A LITTLE BIT OF HISTORY

According to the Middlesex magistrates, gin was 'the principal cause of all the vice and debauchery committed among the inferior sort of people'. Clearly those gentlemen took a robust and not very politically correct view of those making an involuntary and no doubt unwelcome visit to their court back in 1721 …

So things were pretty over-excited in Georgian England, which for most of the early eighteenth century was in the grip of a binge-drinking frenzy we've come to know as the Gin Craze. Daniel Defoe put up a pretty robust defence of the industry though:

> As to the excesses and intemperances of the People, and their drinking immoderate Quantities of Malt Spirits, the Distillers are not concern'd in it at all; their Business is to prepare a Spirit wholesome and good. If the People will destroy themselves by their own Excesses, and make that Poison, which is otherwise an Antidote; 'tis the Magistrates' Business to help that, not the Distillers. (*The Case of the Distillers,* London, 1726)

Mind you, he'd been well paid for that piece of enthusiastic spin-doctoring and was as liable to take the side of the moral majority as defend the distilling industry which, incidentally and apart from some pious sermonising about 'using our products responsibly', hasn't to this day got much further than 'don't blame us if people get off their face on our products'.

You could quite reasonably argue that alcopops and cheap cider are today's equivalent of gin, though as far as I know, no one is yet selling these one shot at a time through a 'Puss and Mew' vending machine. Give them time, though, give them time.

Gin's history begins … well, no one can quite agree. According to some commentators, not least the ever reliable Wikipedia (so it must be true), the Dutch physician Franciscus Sylvius is to be credited with the invention of gin in the mid-seventeenth century.

But 'Dutch Courage' can be dated to 1585 when English troops supported the Dutch army in their war with the Spanish, and there are written references to 'genever' as early as the thirteenth century.

I'm not convinced that it matters. Various nations make various claims for the ancient origins of their national drink; the Scots date whisky to 1494, the Poles claim 1174 for vodka, and the French place Armagnac ahead of cognac with references to 1411. So the English were late to the game with gin, probably sometime in the early seventeenth century. The Worshipful Company of Distillers, Defoe's patron, received its royal warrant in 1638, but the first 'distillers' were actually surgeons, much to the displeasure of the apothecaries who took exception to these upstarts and objected to the dilution of their jealously guarded privileges.

The first attempts at gin were an effort to replicate the genever enjoyed by English troops during their long campaigns in Holland during the Thirty Years' War (1618–1648), but it took the arrival of King William III, or William of Orange as he is better known, in the Glorious Revolution of 1688 for gin to raise its game. And raise it, it did, in response to a series of laws aiming to promote distilling in England (and, not entirely coincidentally, the sale of grain – which suited the landed interest then dominant in Parliament very nicely indeed).

Soon sales of gin exceeded that of the more expensive beer; little wonder when anyone could start distilling by giving ten days' public notice. To the alarm of the genteel and the ruling classes production soared, and in 1729 a licensing system for distillers and publicans was introduced and duty charged. Things got worse: illicitly distilled 'gin' prospered at the expense of legitimate traders. Soon it was estimated that in certain parts of London one private house in four was selling some form of spirits. Regionally the situation was little better and an epidemic of alcohol dependency was taking hold of the poorer parts of the nation.

A further attempt at legislation, the Gin Act of September 1736, merely exacerbated the situation by attempting to restrict retailers and greatly raise the retail price. Though opposed by, among others, the Prime Minister (Sir Robert Walpole) and Dr Samuel Johnson, the law was passed – and then routinely ignored. Only two of the infamous £50 distilling licences (equivalent to around £750,000 today) were taken out, while production is thought to have increased by around half.

Rioting followed the passing of the Act, though street riots by the mob were not infrequent during this period: 1736 saw the Porteous Riots of April and September in Edinburgh, and in east London in July of that year there were riots against the cheap labour of Irish immigrants. A number of pamphlets arguing for and against the measure were issued, some with extravagant titles such as 'An Elegy on the much lamented death of the most excellent, the most truly beloved, and universally admired Lady Madam Geneva'. The lady also appeared in a famous print, 'The Funeral Procession of Madam Geneva'.

Social problems associated with excessive drinking and the public consumption of spirits, such as crime and prostitution, continued, and Parliament, accepting that the 1736 Act was unworkable, returned to the subject in 1742/43. The earlier legislation was abolished and a fairer system of licensing and taxation was introduced, partly following lobbying from the distilling industry. This was further refined in 1747, but the problems remained.

By 1751, the novelist and magistrate Henry Fielding, active in the suppression of the gin trade, attributed to it 'the late (i.e. recent) increase in robbers' and may have worked with or influenced his friend William Hogarth whose pair of engravings 'Gin Lane' and 'Beer Street' dramatically illustrate the scourge of excessive gin drinking in graphic scenes of misery, vice, degradation and death. Hogarth contrasts the squalor resulting from gin consumption with the robust health of the beer drinker, illustrating a street scene where only the pawnbroker's business appears to be suffering. Moralistic verses by the Revd James Townley appear beneath both images; his poem on gin beginning:

Gin, cursed Fiend, with Fury fraught,
Makes human Race a Prey.
It enters by a deadly Draught
And steals our Life away.

But by 1757 the Gin Craze had subsided. In part this was due to the 1751 legislation which required licensees to trade from premises rented for at least £10 a year and thus tended to favour larger, better-quality producers. Historians also point to population growth, poor harvests and the consequent reduction in wages and higher food prices as contributory factors. Gin production simply became less profitable, and so the trade declined until the next boom in Victorian times with the arrival of the gin palace.

These lavish and alluring premises flourished from the late 1820s and provided a vivid contrast to the squalid dram shops that preceded them. Large, dramatically lit and filled with cut-glass and mirrors, they were originally designed for fast service, where the patron was intended to consume his or her drink standing up and then leave to make way for the next customer. Their influence on pub design was profound and they made a notable impact on the novelist Charles Dickens who describes them at length in the *Evening Chronicle* of 19 February 1835:

All is light and brilliancy. The hum of many voices issues from that splendid gin-shop which forms the commencement of the two streets opposite; and the gay building with the fantastically ornamented parapet, the illuminated clock, the plate-glass windows surrounded by stucco rosettes, and its profusion of gas-lights in richly gilt burners, is perfectly dazzling when contrasted with the darkness and dirt we have just left. The interior is even gayer than the exterior. A bar of French-polished mahogany, elegantly carved, extends the whole width of the place; and there are two side-aisles of great casks, painted green and gold, enclosed within a light brass rail, and bearing such inscriptions, as 'Old Tom, 549'; 'Young Tom, 360'; 'Samson, 1421' – the figures agreeing, we presume, with 'gallons', understood. Beyond the bar is a lofty and spacious saloon, full of the same enticing vessels, with a gallery running round it, equally well furnished. On the counter, in addition to the usual spirit apparatus, are two or three little baskets of cakes and biscuits, which are carefully secured at top with wicker-work, to prevent their contents being unlawfully abstracted. Behind it, are two showily dressed damsels with large necklaces, dispensing the spirits and 'compounds'. They are assisted by the ostensible proprietor of the concern, a stout, coarse fellow in a fur cap, put on very much on one side to give him a knowing air, and to display his sandy whiskers to the best advantage.

In his essay, Dickens is highly critical of the prevailing social conditions of the poorer working classes and the unemployed but very well aware of the appeal of the gin palace. He concludes:

> Gin-drinking is a great vice in England, but wretchedness and dirt are a greater; and until you improve the homes of the poor, or persuade a half-famished wretch not to seek relief in the temporary oblivion of his own misery, with the pittance which, divided among his family, would furnish a morsel of bread for each, gin-shops will increase in number and splendour.

Later, in *The Life and Adventures of Martin Chuzzlewit* (1844) we meet the sublime Sairey Gamp: 'The face of Mrs Gamp – the nose in particular – was somewhat red and swollen, and it was difficult to enjoy her society without becoming conscious of a smell of spirits.' It would be some time before gin threw off the stereotype so vividly called up by Dickens.

However, as British imperial power expanded, to become at its zenith the empire on which the sun never set, the medicinal use of quinine to prevent malaria became more widespread. French scientists had extracted quinine from the bark of the cinchona tree in 1817, but the taste was bitter and unpalatable. Soon though, British officers in India, no doubt imbued with patriotic fervour and keen to support domestic industry while helping their medicine go down, hit on the idea of combining it with soda water, sugar, lime and gin.

Thus, as early as 1825 we see the forerunner of the gin and tonic, and gin beginning to move upmarket. Bottles of sweetened quinine water soon appeared and carbonated tonic water was introduced towards the end of the nineteenth century. Meanwhile Johann Schweppe had founded his eponymous business in Vienna in 1783 (he moved to London nine years later). Regardless of the many new brands of tonic now available, some of them excellent, Schweppes must surely be regarded as the most famous name in tonic and is inextricably linked with gin.

Some of the greatest names in gin date from this period, or just earlier. Greenall's was founded in 1761, Gordon's in 1769, and Plymouth in 1793, but with the advent of Tanqueray (1830) and Beefeater (1860s, but building on a firm established some forty years earlier) branding and marketing came to the fore.

Having swept round the British Empire, gin enjoyed its next moment of fame and popularity during the cocktail boom of the Roaring Twenties. Again, it had successfully moved upmarket and was fashionable, acceptable in society and had crossed the Atlantic to conquer America. The advent of Prohibition would not appear to have significantly dented its appeal, with the 'bathtub gin' of legend (and all too often, fact) lending it a brittle glamour and racy charm. The lure of the speakeasy and the blandishments of the bootlegger are an uncomfortable echo of England's Gin Craze.

As late as 1942, Rick (Humphrey Bogart) describes his bar in *Casablanca* as a 'gin joint' – something clandestine, outside the law and carrying the fascination of forbidden fruit.

By the 1950s, however, it had shaken off this raffish clothing and become respectable: now it was something served in golf clubs to the middle-aged and middle-class. Long-established brands began to fail, and old favourites such as Lemon Gin, Orange Gin and Old Tom fell away one by one. Little wonder that within a few short years vodka and white rum would overtake it and gin's slow decline would accelerate. But, as we will see, that was to be reversed even more recently with the arrival of brands such as Bombay (and Bombay Sapphire) and Hendrick's.

Which brings us pretty much up to today, where we find an excitement and energy about gin that has not been seen for more than a hundred years. Today there are probably in excess of 500 brands available worldwide, with more arriving virtually daily.

Sadly, I haven't room for them all – but here are 101 to try before you die!

HOW GIN IS MADE

This is the briefest of descriptions because a number of books and many websites deal with the technical description in great depth and with considerable expertise. Many of the brand entries also expand on aspects of production.

Gin is made from high-strength pure distilled spirits, normally from grain or molasses, which is selected for its clean neutral flavour.

How Gin is made at the
Edinburgh Gin Distillery

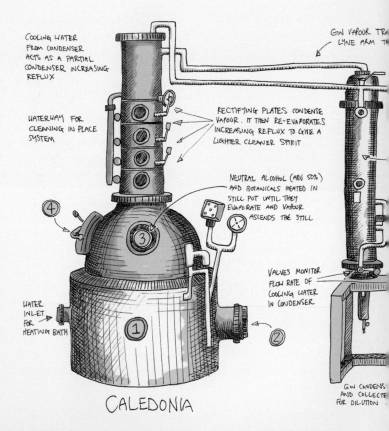

COOLING WATER
FROM CONDENSER
ACTS AS A PARTIAL
CONDENSER INCREASING
REFLUX

WATERWAY FOR
CLEANING IN PLACE
SYSTEM

GIN VAPOUR TR
LYNE ARM T

RECTIFYING PLATES CONDENSE
VAPOUR. IT THEN RE-EVAPORATES
INCREASING REFLUX TO GIVE A
LIGHTER CLEANER SPIRIT

NEUTRAL ALCOHOL (ABV 50%)
AND BOTANICALS HEATED IN
STILL POT UNTIL THEY
EVAPORATE AND VAPOUR
ASCENDS THE STILL

VALVES MONITOR
FLOW RATE OF
COOLING WATER
IN CONDENSER

WATER
INLET
FOR
HEATING BATH

④

③

②

①

GIN CONDENS
AND COLLECTE
FOR DILUTION

CALEDONIA

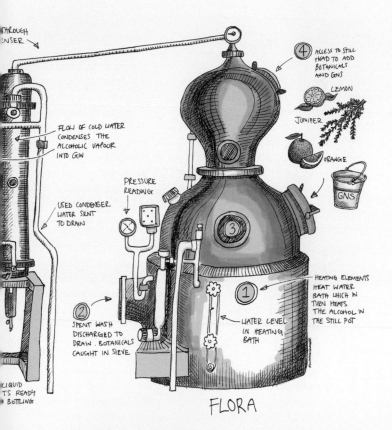

THROUGH
NSER

FLOW OF COLD WATER
CONDENSES THE
ALCOHOLIC VAPOUR
INTO GIN

USED CONDENSER
WATER SENT
TO DRAIN

PRESSURE
READING

④ ACCESS TO STILL
HEAD TO ADD
BOTANICALS
AND GNS

LEMON

JUNIPER

ORANGE

GNS

③

HEATING ELEMENTS
HEAT WATER
BATH WHICH IN
TURN HEATS
THE ALCOHOL IN
THE STILL POT

② SPENT WASH
DISCHARGED TO
DRAIN. BOTANICALS
CAUGHT IN SIEVE

① WATER LEVEL
IN HEATING
BATH

LIQUID
TS READY
BOTTLING

FLORA

Grape-based spirit and, occasionally, beetroot may also be used, though neutral grain spirit (NGS) predominates. In the case of London Dry gin, the best-known style, the neutral spirit is redistilled in the presence of botanicals to give the resultant gin its flavour. Following distillation, nothing is permitted to be added other than neutral alcohol, water to reduce the spirit to bottling strength, and a tiny amount of sugar. 'London' defines the style, and production may take place anywhere: it does not indicate geographical origin

Starting with juniper, which must be its main or characteristic flavour, gin derives its nose and taste from botanicals, which are simply natural herbs and spices such as coriander, orange and lemon peel, cinnamon, nutmeg, angelica and cardamom. Orris root is frequently used in more expensive products, not only for its flavour but because it acts to integrate and bind other flavours together. Botanical recipes, which may be of considerable age, are unique to each brand. These recipes are often a closely guarded secret, though some distillers, commendably in my view, print the details on their bottles or labels. Traditionally, no more than ten or a dozen botanicals would have been used; today, some recipes call for as many as forty-seven different herbs and spices. In recent years there has been a trend for distillers to experiment with ever more exotic or rare botanicals in an effort to develop new flavours and make their product stand out from the crowd.

Distilled gin, often considered a lesser category, is made in a similar way to London gin, but it is permitted to add further flavourings, both natural and artificial, on completion of distillation.

The legal minimum alcohol level in the EU is 37.5% alcohol by volume (abv), although most standard and premium brands are bottled and sold at a higher strength. This, of course, affects the price, not least because duty is charged according to the alcoholic content of the finished product. As gin, unlike whisky or brandy, does not require any maturation it may be bottled immediately, though many brands elect to 'rest' the spirit for some days or weeks to allow all the flavours to integrate fully. There has also been a recent trend to age gin in wooden casks to add colour and further develop flavour.

A third method is 'cold compounding', in which the essential oils from the botanicals are either distilled or simply pressed out and then added to the spirit. The resulting product may be labelled as 'gin', but not 'distilled' or 'London' gin. While in the past this method would have been reserved for cheaper, lower-quality products there are today some more interesting and innovative expressions made in this way by smaller producers.

Brief mention should be made of the cold vacuum method, which often uses a piece of laboratory apparatus known as a rota-vap (rotary evaporator). By distilling under a vacuum, significantly lower temperatures may be used. It is argued that the more subtle and volatile elements of certain botanicals are thereby preserved and the resulting spirit is fresher and more vibrant in taste. A number of smaller producers are making gin in this way.

At the more experimental end of the market, producers are 'finishing' gins in casks previously used for a range of products such as malt whisky and even barrel-aged cocktails. An example is the Batshit Mental range of products, which includes a Negroni-Aged Bathtub Gin. However, such expressions are something of a minority taste, and while they add colour and great variety they account for only a tiny percentage of the global market. Only a few years ago they would have been unthinkable.

Last but not least, it is worth noting that the biggest gin market in the world is the Philippines, accounting for more than 40% of global sales. The local favourite, by a country mile, is Ginebra San Miguel, but, because it is rarely seen beyond its home territory, it doesn't make my 101.

101 GINS

No one really knows how many gin brands are available worldwide (there are probably well over 500), but a selection had to be made. Inevitably it's a personal choice, but I hope that you enjoy my collection and agree that it would make a splendid gin list or back bar.

In the interests of including as many producers as possible, I endeavoured not to list multiple styles of any one single brand, though some expressions seemed so very different or interesting that they were eventually admitted.

For some time I held a strong personal bias in favour of those brands that were actually produced by the principals. It seemed reasonable to prefer companies that made their own products over those that simply went to a contract distiller with a concept or recipe and had some gin made for them, especially as provenance seems likely to become increasingly important. However, I realised that this would not only rule out some very interesting and enjoyable products but that for some fledgling ventures this was their only route to market. Having established their brand, it was clear that some at least would then take the more capital-intensive route of becoming a distiller in their own right. There is more than one example of that in the listings.

While writing this book I quickly lost count of the number of producers, particularly small ones, who assured me of the 'passion' of their founders and wanted to tell me of their 'journey' and the 'hand-crafted' and 'artisanal' nature of their brand, evidently in the belief that this made them stand out in some way. It does not!

In the course of my 'journey' (how I have come to loathe that word) I visited many, many distilleries, some of them very, very large indeed. I did not see any robots making the gin, and master distillers such as Desmond Payne (Beefeater), Tom Nichol (Tanqueray), Nik Fordham (Bombay) and their colleagues in other equally large plants exhibited an enthusiasm, commitment and sheer excitement about their work that was the equal of any neophyte toiling over a forty-litre alembic in an old farm building or inner-city light-industrial unit. They may sell many, many times the volume of their up-and-coming competitors and they may not stick the labels on by hand but the quality of their products and the joy in making them that they freely shared with me should not be underestimated.

My not very original conclusion is that it is the taste that matters!

What follows is presented in a standard format. Next to a large picture of the bottle, there is information on the brand: who owns it; where it is produced (because not all brands are as clear about that as they might be, and it's not unreasonable that you should know where your gin is actually made); what other variants are offered; and where to find more information (almost without exception the brands all have their own websites). There then follows my entirely personal description of what interested me about the particular product: it may be the people, the story, the history, the production method, the packaging or, sometimes, even the taste.

I have not offered scores. These are only ever one man's opinion and I doubt that mine are consistent over time. You may assume that I found the gin drinkable at the very least, otherwise it would not have been included (and there were some that failed at the very first sip) but I don't want my personal preferences and judgements to influence your decision to try any one of these products.

It strikes me that right now there is a great energy pulsing through the world of gin and that this is as good a time as any to learn about it and simply enjoy it. Above all, there is a freshness about gin today that I find extraordinarily invigorating.

I hope that feeling is evident, and that you share it.

And finally, please remember the words of the American writer Roy Blount, Jr: 'A good heavy book holds you down. It's an anchor that keeps you from getting up and having another gin and tonic.'

Time then for our 101 gins.

Photo: Jared Brown

Botanicals ready for distilling at Sipsmith (juniper berries, bottom left).

1

58 GIN

BRAND OWNER: Mark Marmont
DISTILLERY: Hackney Downs Studios, London
WEBSITE: www.58gin.com
VISITOR CENTRE: By arrangement
STRENGTH: 43%
OTHER VARIANTS: Navy Strength, CitroLondon

When I first encountered this in early 2015 it was probably the UK's newest gin brand and I knew at once that it had to go into the book. It's still around and going from strength to strength, so 58 stands as a great example of the new wave of small operations trying to find a gap in the market; it typifies how gin is changing and why it's the most exciting thing on the world spirits scene right now. I know that's a big claim, but read on – by gin number 101, I believe you'll be convinced.

It's the brainchild of Mark Marmont, who describes himself as 'an avid cocktail lover'. He makes just sixty to seventy bottles of gin at a time in a tiny copper pot still in the Hackney Downs Studios, one of the trendier parts of London. Mark did most of the work on the fit-out himself – he has a laboratory background – and after a year of trials, lots of distilling courses and, as he says himself, 'trial and error', he launched 58 with two trial batches.

Mark was fortunate to spend some time living at 58 Colebrooke Row in Angel, just a short stagger from Tony Conigliaro's The Bar With No Name at number 69 (gentleman and bar are legendary in cocktail circles). After sampling many cocktails and realising that the classics are gin-based, he decided to investigate distilling: before long 58 was born. Sometimes the research for this kind of project is brutally demanding and requires a remarkable level of dedication and focus – sometimes it's just great fun.

The 1920s-style logo was developed by Mo Coppoletta, tattoo artist and seriously on-trend guy, as an ode to moonshine and Prohibition and then turned into a finished label in the Hackney Downs Studio by designers Tinder & Sparks. So there are several themes here that exemplify the wave of contemporary gins: a genesis in cocktails; extraordinarily small volumes; individual entrepreneurship and hands-on production. But larger distillers can be, in private at least, somewhat dismissive of their smaller rivals, so is 58 any good?

Well, I think so. There will be batch-to-batch variations of course (all part of the fun and not dissimilar to single cask malt whiskies) but I found it crisp, citrus-y and pleasantly refreshing – great with a dash of Noilly Prat and a twist of lemon peel. More recently, production has been expanded with the limited edition CitroLondon; it's gorgeous, and please, do study the label!

ACHROOUS

BRAND OWNER: Electric Spirit Co. Ltd

DISTILLERY: The Tower Street Stillhouse, Leith, Edinburgh

WEBSITE: www.facebook.com/electricspiritco/

VISITOR CENTRE: No

STRENGTH: 41%

OTHER VARIANTS: None

In the Scotland of my youth there was allegedly a beverage known as 'Electric Soup' – famed, I have to hope, more in legend than fact. Originally said to consist of milk with natural gas bubbled through it, it was the drink of down-and-outs and ne'er-do-wells – the sort of backdoor 'voddie' Rab C. Nesbitt might resort to if he was down on his uppers.

So, Electric Spirit seems a curious name for a distillery in Leith, an area which has recently attained yuppie status by means of some muscular regeneration (i.e. the wholesale demolition of much of the old townscape to be replaced by bland 'designer' flats and a soulless shopping complex). Leith was once the haunt of thirsty sailors on shore leave, legions of accommodating ladies of the night and distraught Hibs fans clinging to fading memories of the Famous Five. Today, it's all five-star foodie restaurants and trendy bars, with just a hint of the delicious possibility of imminent violence to remind one of the Leith of old. Even Hibs win things from time to time these days – but as their hardened fans bitterly observe, it's the hope that kills you.

But the Electric Spirit folks are clearly not shrinking violets, otherwise why put their gin in a day-glo orange bottle (glance left if you don't believe me) and name it Achroous? That's not some strange Scottish war cry, by the way; it's derived from the Ancient Greek for 'colourless', which of course it is. To their eternal credit they also produced a one-off release called Not Another Effing Gin. How I would like to have reviewed that!

Electric Spirit are at the cutting edge of the vibrant Scottish craft distilling scene, and product designer, photographer and distiller James Porteous has worked with juniper, coriander seed, orris root, liquorice root, angelica root, fennel seed and, most notably, Sichuan peppercorns to offer up this most distinctive spiced and complex gin, with attractive citrus and floral notes. Right from their 2015 launch the early batches sold well, allowing Electric Spirit to move to larger premises and acquire a bigger Genio still from Poland.

The Tower Street Stillhouse will also produce Antidote gin for the proposed Port of Leith Distillery. Step back around a hundred years or so, and Leith was a major centre for distillers and wine merchants – how gratifying to see this resurgence of an ancient craft from such a free-thinking, innovative new generation.

ADNAMS COPPER HOUSE

BRAND OWNER: Adnams plc

DISTILLERY: Copper House Distillery, Southwold, Suffolk

WEBSITE: www.adnams.co.uk

VISITOR CENTRE: Yes

STRENGTH: 40%

OTHER VARIANTS: First Rate, Rising Sun

$\mathscr{I}$ suppose that if you've been brewing great beer since 1872 and operate more than seventy pubs and an off-licence chain then starting to distil your own range of spirits isn't the greatest leap in the dark. And with your own outlets to provide a ready market it's probably a sound commercial move, yet it took Adnams until 2010 to start making vodka, gin, whisky and a range of liqueurs.

But, as you'd expect from their reputation as brewers, they've made a pretty decent job of it (I've tasted the whisky in development and it's excellent; I haven't the faintest idea about their vodka as I have a special dispensation never to touch the stuff).

Both vodka and gin start life as unhopped beer from the Adnams brewery. A column still is used to produce the high-strength vodka that then forms the spirit base for the gin. Botanicals (up to thirteen for the premium First Rate style) are added to the beefy 1,000-litre pot and redistilled with no further use of the columns (there is a very clear explanation of this on the website).

The equipment was all new and state-of-the-art when installed in 2009, which is one advantage of starting from scratch, with decent capital behind you. The result is a clean, very elegant and classic London Dry gin that mixes well and has already collected a number of top awards (though as we shall see, not all awards are to be regarded equally highly).

It is, I would judge, more a classic G&T gin than a cocktail base, with a no-nonsense six botanicals; though hibiscus might be considered a bit 'new wave' there is nothing else in there to upset your inner colonel. The higher-strength First Rate employs an additional eight botanicals but drops the hibiscus, thus making thirteen in all. However, to be honest, I preferred Copper House

If you get the chance to visit Southwold grab it and do not let go. After you've visited the brewery and distillery (there are various tours to take) the town itself is quite charming; the beach huts are fun to ogle (especially after you realise the prices at which they change hands); and the pier is worth the trip on its own. You can get great fish; you're only a few miles from Snape Maltings for some culture; and sitting on the beach at Southwold, gin and tonic in hand, watching the rolling waves and passing clouds is one of the great pleasures in life.

ALDI'S OLIVER CROMWELL

BRAND OWNER: Aldi Stores Ltd

DISTILLERY: not disclosed

WEBSITE: www.aldi.co.uk

VISITOR CENTRE: Lots of shops – not quite the same though

STRENGTH: 37.5%

OTHER VARIANTS: Boyle's Irish, Victoria Pink, Needle

'*What* do you think you're doing?' I asked my son, who was making sloe gin. 'You've picked all this nice fruit and now you're sticking some horrid supermarket cheapie in there. I trust you don't expect me to drink that.' Being a bit of a drinks snob.

'No, it's OK actually,' he replied. 'You should try it.' And so I did. And then I had another (you should always listen to your children). And I found it good – really not at all bad.

Try to imagine that this doesn't come in a bottle that's a pallid imitation of a well-known brand leader. Try to forget it costs around a tenner a bottle. Imagine if you will, that it's distilled in a former railway arch in Shoreditch by some bearded hipster sporting an armful of tattoos, and costs at least thirty quid. For a 50cl bottle.

Or run up by a radical extreme cocktail commune in a disused monastery in Oregon using organic juniper gathered by moonlight by barefoot monks. At 3,000 feet.

Or simply decant it into a smarter bottle and then amaze your mates. After a while you'll forget your preconceptions and just enjoy a well-made product that lets the liquid do the talking. It's a lovely light and undemanding product (I don't mean that in any pejorative sense), crisp, refreshing and well balanced.

Aldi's Oliver Cromwell Gin was awarded the only Gold Medal in the standard gin class by *Spirits Business* magazine and, even more impressively, another Gold in the International Spirits Challenge (both 2014). These awards followed a 2013 Silver Medal from the IWSC judges, who are not easily pleased. So you don't have to take my (or my son's) word for it: this really is much, much better than the price and packaging would suggest.

If I was being picky I'd like to see the strength somewhat higher, but then I have to remember the price. For the money you can pour with a liberal hand. This looks even more impressive if you have poured it into a trendier bottle and your guests think they're getting the £30 stuff. Believe me, they will.

There's something else you should know about Aldi: its white chocolate is utterly delicious. I realise that's got nothing whatsoever to do with gin, but it's a good tip.

ANNO

BRAND OWNER:	Anno Distillers Ltd
DISTILLERY:	Anno, Marden, Kent
WEBSITE:	www.annodistillers.co.uk
VISITOR CENTRE:	Yes
STRENGTH:	43%
OTHER VARIANTS:	Sixty Squared, Sloe

Anno is part of the new wave of craft distillers, but not entirely typical. It isn't run by some tattooed hipsters but by two more senior (in age and career terms) former scientists from the pharmaceutical industry who have established something of a family enterprise. What's more, they don't appear to be trying to reinvent gin. Rather, they work within the classic parameters while offering something distinctive.

And, to their credit, they appear to have created something a little bit different and unusual for their first offering. To judge by their website they have approached the whole operation with some precision and rigour, first commissioning their own unique still design from Christian Carl and then selecting quite unfamiliar local Kent botanicals to give Anno its own personality and flavour.

The first time that I tried it I thought that under the classic juniper aromas I could detect a slightly salty tang. It's certainly spicy with some sweet citrus hints, but it's also very well balanced and quite elegant in style with a consistent finish. I still thought there was an elusive salty note in there, which was rather intriguing, so I checked the botanicals and found that they use Kentish samphire. Now, according to the distillery, this should lend 'a rather pleasant sweetness about it with fresh grassy notes'. I daresay they're right and I just imagined it, but I was nonetheless rather gratified to make an association with saltiness and then find samphire in there – which is agreeably salty when eaten of course.

Also in the botanical basket – they employ one for the more delicate ingredients – are Kentish hops, lavender and elderflower, along with rose hips, chamomile and three different citrus components. There's a full list of all sixteen on the website, which is a model of clarity and ease of operation by the way.

They've also managed to create a clean, distinctive and appealing look to the bottle with graphics applied directly to the glass in place of a conventional label. The distinctive 'A' symbol is very strong and relates not only to a name derived from the two co-founders (ANdy and NOrman) but is actually taken from an ancient German alchemical text where it was used as the symbol to describe the process of distillation.

I like the link with the early alchemists, proto-scientists who sought to turn base metals into gold, and these Kentish pioneers, applying modern scientific methodology to a time-honoured tradition while investing it with some of their own restless curiosity.

AUDEMUS PINK PEPPER

BRAND OWNER:	Audemus Spirits
DISTILLERY:	4 Rue du Pont Faumet, Cognac 16100, France
WEBSITE:	www.audemus-spirits.com
VISITOR CENTRE:	Visits possible by special arrangement
STRENGTH:	44%
OTHER VARIANTS:	Old Ma's Port Barrel Aged

Any company based in the very heart of Cognac, founded by an Australian and managed by two fellows styling themselves Director of Capers and Director of Doing, must be worthy of consideration, even though the distillery is a mere five years old. Despite that, it has made quite an impact on the French craft distilling scene, attracting the attention of the more innovative cocktail mixologists and collecting major awards in international competition.

What we find is quite an unusual set-up: separate reduced pressure; low temperature distillation of each ingredient (rather like Sacred); and the use of some unconventional botanicals. These include honey (rather like Dodd's), vanilla, tonka beans and the pink peppercorns that give the gin its name.

Distiller Miko Abouaf (he's the Australian by the way and the Director of Capers – not the salty little berries often found in cooking but suggestive of frivolity and jolly larking about) had spent some time working in Cognac but wanted to create his own aromatic gin built upon a juniper base. His goal was to create a product with a complexity that will develop and evolve over time, both in bottle and in the glass.

The juniper base gives the gin a classical integrity but other notes emerge. The tonka beans enhance the effect of the vanilla (I'll admit here that I had to look those beans up as I'd never heard of the things) and, served at room temperature or gently warmed, the overall impact is delightfully reminiscent of a fragrant pâtisserie: certainly a gin that you can sip with pleasure.

But served over ice or in a suitable cocktail, spicy notes from juniper and cardamom are more obviously apparent. This is where the pink peppercorn comes in, but first understand that the name is something of a misnomer: this is actually a dried berry fruit. However, it does look rather like a peppercorn once dried and has something of a peppery taste, hence its title.

Audemus is not the only distiller using this botanical – both Durham Gin and Tarquin's in the UK are fans – but it is somewhat unorthodox. As it grows wild in Australia, perhaps it was a taste of home for Miko but whatever the reason for its inclusion it certainly works well here, balancing the warmth and smooth mouthfeel of the locally sourced honey. A very impressive product, and attractively presented.

BATHTUB

BRAND OWNER:	Atom Supplies Ltd
DISTILLERY:	Prof. Cornelius Ampleforth's Compounding Works, Tunbridge Wells
WEBSITE:	www.ableforths.com
VISITOR CENTRE:	No
STRENGTH:	43.3%
OTHER VARIANTS:	Navy Strength, Old Tom, Sloe, Cask Aged, Cask Aged Navy

If nothing else, you've got to admit this is unusual. But stick with me; it's also tasty.

Once upon a time there was a Professor Cornelius Ampleforth who fulfilled a lifelong ambition with the release of his extraordinary Bathtub Gin. Not content with this highly successful experiment, he proceeded to lock himself back inside his laboratory and set about all manner of additional, exciting projects. The result was an entire range of original and re-imagined spirits inspired by modern technology and bygone eras alike. Whether it's cold compounding or distillation under vacuum, the madcap professor does whatever it takes to produce the finest libations and retain the freshness of the wonderful botanicals he uses. Or so they say . . .

I'll let you into a secret: there isn't really a Professor Ampleforth (sorry if you're disappointed), but if it helps, think of him as a sort of Santa Claus of gin, showering us with all kinds of goodies. The range, which keeps growing, is the brainchild of a well-known, dynamic and irreverent web-based drinks retailer who consistently surprise with their very different offerings.

But something strange has happened. All mention of the benevolent professor has disappeared and now the label reads 'Ableforth'. Perhaps Colonel Mustard did for him in the library with a candlestick . . . we may never know.

But his legacy lives on in products conceived to explore and showcase different aspects of gin's personality. Cold compounding would generally be sniffed at as the lowest form of gin manufacture, normally used for the cheapest (and not very nice) products. Rather more care is taken here, and anyway, many of the products are cold vacuum-distilled, which is rather different, more complex and technically demanding. So, underneath the carefully cultivated offbeat image is a well thought-out set of varying expressions from a young and enthusiastic team who truly care about what they are doing (while trying not to show it too obviously, which is quite an English attitude if you think about it).

And, if my word's not good enough, Bathtub Gin keeps winning awards – more than I could be bothered to count. So that's not bad for a mad professor from Tunbridge Wells (I think he does exist but they've locked him in the attic 'cos they're jealous).

BECKETT'S

BRAND OWNER: Kingston Distillers Ltd

DISTILLERY: Kingston Distillers Ltd,
28 Portsmouth Road,
Kingston upon Thames, London

WEBSITE: www.beckettsgin.co.uk

VISITOR CENTRE: No

STRENGTH: 40%

OTHER VARIANTS: Sloe

One of the loveliest things about loving gin at the moment is that you can enjoy your favourite tipple *and* a glow of virtue. Gins – well, some gins – have a social conscience. One shares its profits to help gorillas and another to protect elephants.

In this case, charity begins at home: Beckett's, which uses hand-picked juniper berries from Box Hill in Surrey (the setting, you will recall, for a famous if unhappy picnic in Jane Austen's *Emma*), is working with the National Trust, Forest Research and Natural England to help save juniper from extinction in England. A worthy cause, you may feel, and one close to the heart of all true gin lovers. If it works, juniper will once again flourish on Juniper Top, Surrey.

For a relatively new company, launching its signature gin as recently as 2014, this is a bold and noteworthy initiative, giving it bragging rights as the only gin made using English juniper. It is, however, a necessarily small-scale operation, hence there is no visitor centre or access to the distillery. As founder Neil Beckett explains, this is 'a home-based business so there are no plans to have visitors until we relocate'.

The other distinctive note here comes from the use of Kingston upon Thames mint as a botanical – sweet yet cooling, it harmonises with just four other ingredients in a deceptively simple formula that results in a mix of zesty citrus (lime and sweet orange peel) and earthy spice (orris and coriander). Mint is the recommended garnish, as perhaps it should be; it's grown at the distillery's home.

There's a puzzling reference on the label to 'Type 1097'. Surely they didn't have 1,096 prior attempts at the recipe? I knew you'd want to know, so I enquired and the answer is that it is their first gin (hence 1) and this was the ninety-seventh attempt to perfect the recipe. I don't suppose 'Type 197' has quite the same ring to it!

More figures: there are now at least twenty-four gin distilleries working in London. That's a remarkable revival and Beckett's is a worthy addition to their number. And another: there may have been ninety-six steps on the way to the final formula, but there were eighteen label design concepts developed by their designers – in Surrey, naturally.

Local juniper; local mint; local artwork; your cash helps save English juniper and the brand even sponsors a gin quiz at local gastropub the Lass O'Richmond Hill. Splendid stuff.

9

BEEFEATER DRY

BRAND OWNER: Pernod Ricard

DISTILLERY: Beefeater, Kennington, London

WEBSITE: www.beefeatergin.com

VISITOR CENTRE: Yes

STRENGTH: 40%

OTHER VARIANTS: Beefeater 24, London Garden (distillery exclusive), London Pink, Burrough's Reserve

Since 2005, when the French drinks giant Pernod Ricard acquired the Beefeater brand and distillery, things have been looking up for this great old brand – for years the last branded flag-carrier for London-distilled London Dry. They've poured both money and love (the latter every bit as important as the cash) into developing both distillery and brand. Their urbane and unflappable master distiller Desmond Payne is clearly loving every moment of this well-deserved highpoint in his distinguished gin career.

But gin lovers have long recognised the quality behind its iconic label (though, as an aside, I do wish the restless young people in marketing would stop messing about with their torrent of 'limited edition' label designs – if it ain't broke, don't fix it). In many ways, this would be the gin I'd recommend to someone who only had room for one gin in their cupboard and was watching the pennies. Frankly, it's great value, and all things considered it's hard to beat for an authentic gin taste. While researching and writing this book I used it as my reference point.

Recently the distillery has benefited from the development of a small but rather handsome visitor centre (£12, but that includes a G&T) which traces the history of gin, with particular emphasis on London's role, naturally. If you're sufficiently interested you can investigate the individual exhibits with the assistance of an iPad, or you can just stroll quickly through to the tasting that awaits. In the inevitable shop you can pick up a bottle of Beefeater's harder-to-find expressions including the premium 24 (45% with extra tea and citrus botanicals), Burrough's Reserve, a 'barrel rested' aged gin distilled in a tiny nineteenth-century copper still, and the distillery exclusive London Garden expression, inspired, or so it is said, by a visit to the Chelsea Physic Garden. That's the one I'd pick if I could only take one home with me, but all have a claim to your wallet.

In recent years there have also been interesting summer and winter limited editions. You might find one in a bar that keeps a decent range of gins. They're well worth trying and, if you're very lucky, there may even be some bottles left in a few specialist outlets.

Ubiquitous it may be but Beefeater is a classic. Until you've tried it you're not really a gin drinker.

10

BERRY BROS. & RUDD LONDON DRY

BRAND OWNER: Berry Bros. & Rudd

DISTILLERY: Thames Distillers, Timbermill Distillery, Clapham, London

WEBSITE: www.bbr.com

VISITOR CENTRE: No, but a lovely shop at 3 St James's Street, Mayfair, London

STRENGTH: 40.6%

OTHER VARIANTS: None

A blast from the past? After all, what more traditional, upper-crust symbol of London could one find than Berry Bros. & Rudd's delightfully antiquated shop at 3 St James's Street in the very heart of Mayfair? Over three centuries of tradition seep from its storied walls. They have long supplied the British ruling classes' thirst with claret and other fine beverages, and were responsible for creating Cutty Sark, one of the great cocktail whiskies.

So naturally they have a gin. In the last edition I featured their traditional, juniper-led No. 3 London Dry. But there's a slight problem. The bottle gives the hint, for it's in the shape of an old-fashioned genever. Which hails from the Low Countries, not London. And it turns out that this very fine, inimitably English gin is, in fact, distilled for Berry's in Holland, which, of course, is where gin's story started (unless, perchance, you buy the Malfy story – see entry 61).

However, now – drum roll, please – they offer a London Dry *actually made in London*. And it's my 'blast from the past' because this is a recreation of Berrys' Best, the gin they were selling as long ago as 1909 and a product highly praised by David Embury (a giant amongst cocktail writers) as representing 'superior British gin production'. But it was a casualty of gin's sorry decline after the Second World War and only one bottle survived in BB&R's hallowed cellars.

Could it be cloned? They turned to Master Distiller Charles Maxwell, modest gin superstar and the man behind many of the smaller brands that have recently flooded the market. With one tiny sample to work with, Maxwell's venerable John Dore stills – Tom Thumb and Thumbelina (London-made, naturally) – were soon in action and the legend was reborn.

This is a taste of history, a juniper-y London Dry classic. Forget exotic fruit infusions; eschew lengthy lists of obscure botanicals; shun the capricious and wilfully neoteric; this is the gin that our forefathers drank (always assuming they could afford to shop at Berry Bros.). Great decisions that affected the fate of nations were likely made over large London Dry G&Ts in the more exclusive recesses of London's clubland, for this truly reeked of privilege.

No longer. In our more democratic age this is a little bit of a bargain: a good tenner cheaper than their No. 3 and made in London to boot. Hip, hip, hooray!

11

BLUECOAT

BRAND OWNER: Samson & Surrey LLC
DISTILLERY: Philadelphia Distilling,
Philadelphia, Pennsylvania, USA
WEBSITE: www.bluecoatgin.com
VISITOR CENTRE: Yes
STRENGTH: 47%
OTHER VARIANTS: Barrel Reserve, Elderflower

Bluecoat is a perfect example of the new contenders that are revitalising gin's image – and taste. Using their own custom-designed still, specially crafted in Scotland, Philadelphia Distilling have aimed from the get-go to make what they call American Dry Gin, in a style that is all their own. For a small start-up the company have enjoyed some considerable success and, though they concentrate on the US market, supplies have made it to the UK.

Their neutral grain spirit is re-distilled five times in their pot still and the use of organic American juniper provides an earthy base to the nose and flavour, while the distinctive signature of Bluecoat is a citrus note derived (I believe) from grapefruit peel, though the distiller would neither confirm nor deny my theory.

Though now part of the Samson & Surrey boutique spirits operation, the company is still largely run by the energetic and committed original team who were pioneering and enthusiastic enough to establish Pennsylvania's first legal distillery since Prohibition. Based first in an industrial unit on the edge of the city, they have since moved all their distilling and bottling operations to a new, larger site located in the hipster neighbourhood of Fishtown – 'the hottest neighbourhood in the USA' according to a recent issue of *Forbes* magazine – and opened a visitor centre. Enlightened new legislation makes it possible to retail their products direct to the public and offer distillery tours – vital promotional activity for a company of this scale.

Having had the opportunity to visit both sites, I'm impressed by what has been done in their new home and the impact it's having in the regeneration of a distinctly gritty part of town.

The Bluecoat name emphasises the distinctively American nature of this gin, being based on the nickname of the militia of the American War of Independence (or Revolutionary War, as the beastly colonists insist on calling it), hence the company's slogan 'Be Revolutionary'. It's very far from revolting, though, and even a true Brit can enjoy Bluecoat's cleansing, refreshing taste and 47% abv strength. The Barrel Reserve is a small-batch release, aged in American oak barrels for three months, which are used only twice. I find the slightly fuller flavour works agreeably well in a Negroni, and look out too for the zesty Elderflower expression as Bluecoat expand into international markets.

12

BOMBAY SAPPHIRE

BRAND OWNER: Bacardi

DISTILLERY: Bombay Spirits Company,
Laverstoke, Hampshire

WEBSITE: www.bombaysapphire.com

VISITOR CENTRE: Yes

STRENGTH: 40%

OTHER VARIANTS: Original Dry, Star of Bombay

Like a number of other currently fashionable gins, Bombay Sapphire relies on its retro-style packaging to persuade us it's been around for ages. In one sense it has, in that the base recipe (as used in the Original Dry variant) dates back to 1761 when it was known as Warrington Dry Gin. It did not appear in its Bombay guise until 1960, and Sapphire, which added two botanicals to the recipe, was launched only in 1987.

It has a decent claim to saving the entire gin category, here and in the USA. A new wave of innovative bartenders, led by the legendary Dick Bradsell (inventor of the Bramble cocktail and mentor to today's tattooed 'mixologists'), picked up on Sapphire's light, fresh and delicate nose and taste, and began to look at gin in an exciting new way.

It took a little while for this to gather momentum but a number of competitors followed, chief amongst them Hendrick's. Today, it seems that new gins, ultimately inspired by Sapphire, appear almost weekly.

In 1997 the brand was acquired by Bacardi. Until 2014 production remained at Warrington, where it was distilled under contract by G&J Greenall, but today it has its own home at the splendid Laverstoke Mill, where a magnificent visitor centre has been built. I'll simply urge you to go without delay.

There you can stroll through the very attractive grounds; gasp at the soaring glasshouses designed by Thomas Heatherwick; learn all about botanicals; design your own cocktail; but, best of all, see the highly unusual Carterhead stills which aim to preserve the fresh character of the botanicals through the vapour infusion method of distilling. The result is a subtle and delicate spirit, which, though light in character, does not lack for complexity or charm. Production has been greatly expanded by the multi-million pound move to Laverstoke but great care has been taken to ensure absolute continuity of flavour.

Today, there are a number of variants. Original Dry has been relaunched in the UK, but at the reduced strength of 37.5% abv – a mistake in my view as it drinks disappointingly thin. What you really want is the export strength Sapphire (47%) as found at the airport, which is a superbly rewarding component of a good cocktail, or the exotic Star of Bombay with its beguiling pepper and lemongrass notes.

Then you can raise a glass to the gin which, almost single-handedly, rescued gin!

13

BOTANIST

BRAND OWNER: Rémy Cointreau

DISTILLERY: Bruichladdich, Islay

WEBSITE: www.thebotanist.com

VISITOR CENTRE: Yes

STRENGTH: 46%

OTHER VARIANTS: None

This is what happens when a small, rather isolated whisky distillery that is not without a sense of its own importance makes gin. It's lovely!

The Botanist is made on Islay by Bruichladdich – self-styled 'progressive Hebridean distillers'. They do bang on a bit about how they're different from everyone else – though it's also fair to acknowledge that in many ways they are. Their near-obsessive fans have awarded them cult status, despite the distillery and brands having been sold in July 2012 to the French group Rémy Cointreau. In recent years they've shed the *enfant-terrible* pose, which was getting a trifle wearing (at least I thought so) and have matured somewhat.

But they still do fun, unexpected and offbeat things, and for that we may forgive them a lot. Such an attitude lay behind their last-minute recovery of one of the very few surviving true Lomond stills left anywhere in the world shortly before it was fated to end as scrap. The Lomond still was originally designed in the late 1950s as a sort of compromise between a pot still and a column still and was intended for Scotch whisky. For all sorts of reasons it never really worked satisfactorily and, like the dustbin it resembles, was destined for the waste-basket of whisky history.

However, Bruichladdich's master distiller Jim McEwan realised that if run very slowly it could be ideal for making gin. As the distillery was casting around for new, cash-generative products gin was duly made. But, ever curious, McEwan adapted the still to include a separate container for the botanicals (sourced, of course, uniquely on Islay) and thus worked the Lomond apparatus as a sort of hybrid Carterhead. It's not, let it be said, a particularly good-looking piece of kit. In fact, the distillery have affectionately named it Ugly Betty and painted a rather voluptuous lady onto the top of the column (she's not at all ugly).

As for the gin itself, they first use a fairly standard range of botanicals which are infused with the base spirit and then augment these by passing the vapour through a further twenty-two more delicate island botanicals. The result is a complex, robust yet floral gin of great charm. Rémy Cointreau bought Bruichladdich for their single malt whisky – they may come to find that this was the real bargain.

14

BOXER

BRAND OWNER: Green Box Drinks Ltd

DISTILLERY: The Langley Distillery, Langley Green, Warley, West Midlands

WEBSITE: www.boxergin.com

VISITOR CENTRE: No

STRENGTH: 40%

OTHER VARIANTS: None

You think this is called Boxer because there's a picture of a boxer on the bottle, don't you? Well, it might be . . . but I have another theory. It may just be that it's because it comes *in a box*. Clever, eh?

Not for you and me, you understand; we just get it in a bottle, like any old other gin, and, as you'd expect, there is indeed an illustration of two strapping fellows engaged in fisticuffs right there on the front. But if you run a bar and order Boxer, the first order comes conventionally packaged but your second and subsequent orders arrive as a 4.2-litre bag in a box (like a wine box but bigger – 4.2 litres is the equivalent of the trade's standard six-bottle case). Why?

Well, Green Box Drinks point out that producing a new glass spirits bottle produces 630g of CO_2, and the amount of energy saved by refilling one bottle could power a 100-watt light bulb for eleven hours. The box of Boxer reduces packaging by 95%, they say, transported weight by 45% and transported volume by 63%. All you have to do as the bar owner is keep your empties, carefully refill them (there's a panel on the box where you note how many bottles have been drawn off from the bag), and sit back luxuriating sanctimoniously in a sense of your green virtue. I'm not aware of any other company doing this but it may be a trend that we will see more of in the future.

However, it may be green, but is it any good? Well, if you like a pronounced juniper hit on your gin, then yes it is. Boxer separately distil fresh wild juniper berries at source in the Himalayas and cold-press their bergamot peel and add these extracts to a classic London Dry gin distilled by Langley's of Birmingham (their renowned 'Angela' still is in action here). This means it may only be described as a 'distilled gin' but it ensures a very fresh, forceful and vibrant delivery of the key flavours, which are long-lasting and stand up well to dilution with tonic or in a cocktail.

Sipped neat, the flavours in Boxer are perhaps too assertive, so this is something of a heavyweight amongst gins – to borrow a memorable phrase, it floats like a butterfly but stings like a bee.

Meanwhile, don't forget about Langley's who we shall meet again. They're an important part of gin's revival.

15

BRIGHTON

BRAND OWNER: Brighton Spirits Company
DISTILLERY: The Urchin, Hove
WEBSITE: www.brightongin.com
VISITOR CENTRE: You could visit The Urchin
STRENGTH: 40%
OTHER VARIANTS: None

The late, great Keith Waterhouse, a long-time resident, once memorably declared that 'Brighton has the air of a town helping the police with its inquiries'. It certainly carries a certain raffish manner, an insouciant attitude and a tawdry glamour that for years marked it out as the place to go for a dirty weekend, or perhaps for ill-matched couples needing to provide sham proof of adultery to obtain a divorce.

Again and again this image occurs in books: from *Pride and Prejudice* by way of *Vanity Fair*, *Brighton Rock* and *Sugar Rush* Brighton acts as a counterpoint to London, a veritable den of iniquity, sexual excess and casual violence. Not, I hasten to add, that anything at all exciting has ever happened to me on my all too fleeting visits ('and a jolly good thing, too' adds Mrs Buxton).

Gin seems Brighton's natural partner; what else would you drink on some illicit liaison than Mother's Ruin? So it's perhaps surprising that no one has thought to launch a Brighton Gin until now. Even if it were distilled somewhere else Brighton's glitzy allure would surely have exercised a fascination for even the most *outré* of drinkers and injected a *soupçon* of hitherto unsuspected debauchery into the image of the most drably respectable of provincial chartered accountants. But it seems not, so it fell to a group of five Brighton chums to make the first move and distil their very own gin beside the seaside.

So, with their second-hand still, Kathy Caton, former restaurateur, Dr Ian Barry, physicist turned distiller, Helen Chesshire, first lady of drinks PR, Jonathan Ray, drinks journalist, and one-time brewery and coffee entrepreneur Nigel Lambe decided it had to be done. Loving Brighton as they do, the cheery labelling, with its hints of the fairground, has been inspired by the city itself and the distinctive Brighton seafront blue that appears on railings and bus shelters. Was that risky or simply *risqué*?

Their first run of 400 bottles apparently flew off the shelves. The aim is to build local support and then expand, though by the time this reaches the bookshops I fully expect that this crisp citrus-led gin, with its secret botanicals (though they do admit to fresh orange, angelica, lime and the liver-cleansing milk thistle), will have achieved success far from the seaside.

Finally, then, something you can bring home from London-by-the-Sea that you can safely share with your mother-in-law.

16

BROKER'S

BRAND OWNER:	Broker's Gin Ltd, London
DISTILLERY:	The Langley Distillery, Langley Green, Warley, West Midlands
WEBSITE:	www.brokersgin.com
VISITOR CENTRE:	No
STRENGTH:	40%
OTHER VARIANTS:	Export Strength

Does anyone still wear a bowler hat? Isn't the little plastic hat on top of this bottle, and even the name, simply a bit of a gimmick? Well, yes, but then the company themselves shamelessly admit that this is 'a brand with personality and playfulness; a quirky marketing approach'.

And what's wrong with a bit of fun, you might ask. At under twenty quid this would make a splendid present (I wouldn't turn it down). If you splash out just a little more, you can afford their 47% export strength but check the label carefully if that's not what you want; they are very similarly packaged and easily confused (until you start drinking, that is).

But is the gin any good, I hear you cry. Well, if awards are anything to go by, then yes it is. My bottle came with a little leaflet proudly emblazoned with the unambiguous words 'World's Best Gin' that inside listed a string of medals going back to 2007. If you're not convinced, the website has a longer list going back to 2000. On top of this impressive claim, they go on to assert that Broker's has won more top awards in international competitions over the last ten years than any other gin.

Others might dispute that, but the problem here for the unwitting consumer is that brands have entered into a sort of arms race and, spotting an opportunity, lots of new awards have sprung up, happy to collect the entry fees and dish out gongs. Not all awards are of equal merit – you wouldn't consider a win in the one hundred yards at a school parents' day to match Olympic gold – and the same applies to drinks awards.

Not, I rush to say, that Broker's is anything other than a completely splendid and very fine libation, especially if you like a straightforward, traditional classic gin which this is, most definitely and unapologetically. Distilled by Langley's in 'Angela', a good old John Dore pot still of a century and more's vintage, just ten botanicals are used. No surprises and nothing 'weird and wonderful' in the list; after all, as they say themselves, 'We believe our forefathers did an unbeatable job perfecting gin recipes over many hundreds of years.'

That seems fair enough. So, if you're looking for a slightly offbeat gift for a gin connoisseur that won't break the bank look no further. Broker's is it: you can take your hat off to it.

BROOKLYN

BRAND OWNER:	Brooklyn Craft Works
DISTILLERY:	Warwick Valley Winery & Distillery, Warwick, New York State
WEBSITE:	www.brooklyngin.com
VISITOR CENTRE:	No
STRENGTH:	40%
OTHER VARIANTS:	None

Hipper even than Tooting, surely Brooklyn, New York, is the epitome of cool. Founded in 2010, the intention has always been to distil in the city, but, for the present, financial pressures mean that Brooklyn's production and bottling takes place at the Warwick Valley Distillery in Hudson Valley. But don't ever confuse it with Breuckelen gin which *is* distilled in Brooklyn – this being the land of the free, lawyers were soon involved in a spat over naming rights. Potato, potahto …

But since Brooklyn are hardly the only brand working with a third-party distillery, I think we can let them off this minor geographic infelicity, especially as Warwick Valley was the first distillery to be licensed in New York State since Prohibition. This is a great example of American gin – loads of citrus (think Bluecoat) as they pack the Carl still with key limes, kumquat, lemon, lime and orange, stressing that the fruit is fresh and hand-peeled. And while on the hand-crafted note it would be remiss not to note that the Albanian juniper berries are cracked by hand as well – these guys must have a firm handshake – so if initially a little subdued the pine note is there: take a second sip and enjoy the subtle segue from citrus-led to juniper influence. Clever stuff.

Refreshingly, given the trend for the early pioneers to sell up, Brooklyn remains independent in ownership, but despite the inevitable constraints this involves have achieved decent international distribution. Part of that success must be attributed to the very striking packaging: the heavy, green-tinted art deco-style bottle with its prominent bronze medallion really stands out on shelf and is satisfying to hold and pour (but it is heavy, so watch out). It's understated but authoritative.

Hailing from the USA, this just has to work in cocktails and, no surprise, Brooklyn really hits its stride here. The website offers a helpful range and you shouldn't hesitate to experiment. It packs more of a punch than the 40% strength would suggest, with the pronounced citrus note holding up well after mixing.

Brooklyn has a hatful of worthwhile awards to its name, including double golds at both the San Francisco World Spirits Competition and the New York World Wine & Spirits Competition to put alongside various craft distilling accolades. It's decent value for the presentation and with all that citrus fruit at under £40 it's definitely one to look out for.

18

BURLEIGH'S

BRAND OWNER: 45 West Distillers

DISTILLERY: Nanpantan, Loughborough, Leicestershire

WEBSITE: www.burleighsgin.com

VISITOR CENTRE: Yes

STRENGTH: 40%

OTHER VARIANTS: Export Strength, Distiller's Cut, Pink Edition, Leicester Dry (LCFC)

I've just noticed that a lot of gins begin with the letter 'B'. Before you ask, I haven't the faintest idea why this is, but look how long it's taken us just to get here. What's more, Burleigh's is distilled by a chap named Baxter. Call it coincidence if you will, but I think it's fate.

He appears to be moving backwards from the letter 'C'. That's not a cryptic clue, merely a reference to the fact that Burleigh's master distiller Jamie Baxter began work at Chase Distillery, then moved on to City of London and continues in a consultancy capacity helping other smaller distillers get started.

Right now, he's got his own distillery (with custom-designed still, naturally) at the wonderfully named Nanpantan and, with partners Graham Veitch, Tim Prime and Phil Burley, has created Burleigh's. Now, you might assume that it's Burleigh's for Mr Burley, but you'd be wrong – the name comes from the distillery's location near to Charnwood Forest and Burleigh Wood nature reserve. As the story goes, Jamie was walking there one day and was inspired by the local botanicals that he found – including silver birch, dandelion, burdock, elderberry and a few secret ingredients as well as some more conventional ones.

As a mark of how fast the new generation of artisan gins are gaining acceptance, only two months after producing its first batch Burleigh's was seen on the shelves of Harrods and the Savoy along with the two Michelin star Hand and Flowers, in Marlow, Buckinghamshire. It's impressive stuff.

As to the signature expression, it's a fairly classic London Dry, well made and elegant. The nose is crisp, clean and fresh, with juniper and citrus coming through nice and early, an initial hit of juniper and pine with floral and spicy dry notes on tasting, followed by tart orange notes and a warming finish.

And, if you're inspired, you can tap into this expertise, because 45 West offer a full service to help you set up your own distillery, right down to sending in a 'flying distiller' every few batches once you've got started, just to hold your hand until everything is going smoothly. So they're not frightened of competition, it would seem, but some of their competitors might get a surprise, especially if they go down to the woods today. Making gin is no picnic!

19

CAORUNN

BRAND OWNER: Inver House Distillers

DISTILLERY: Balmenach, Cromdale, Moray

WEBSITE: www.caorunngin.com

VISITOR CENTRE: No

STRENGTH: 41.8%

OTHER VARIANTS: None

An apple a day keeps the doctor away!' Well, that's my excuse. Caorunn (say it 'ka-roon') recommend a slice of red apple in place of the more normal lime or lemon and I think that's probably a first. Is it just a gimmick, though?

Well, if lime or lemon are there to enhance gin's citrus flavours, the fact that Caorunn include the ancient Coul Blush variety of apples in their botanical line-up, alongside six classics such as juniper and coriander, could provide the justification. Mind you, they've got rowanberries in there as well (the trees keep witches away, at least according to Celtic folk tradition – and ever since I planted one I've never had a problem with over-friendly old hags at my front door), and bog myrtle and heather, not to mention dandelion. Quite apart from the fact that dandelion is a pernicious weed, albeit with a pretty flower, I believe we'll draw a veil over its alleged diuretic properties. I'm not at all certain what I'm expected to taste when encountering dandelion, though as we have already noted, it's also used in Burleigh's gin.

By virtue of its parent Inver House Distillers, who have a range of single malt whiskies, Caorunn have achieved wider distribution than many other small gin brands. They've also collected a number of decent awards. What's more interesting is that it's made at Balmenach, a small single malt whisky distillery on Speyside that dates back to 1824, but using a dedicated gin still. Around 1,000 litres of triple-distilled grain spirit are used in each batch, the spirit vapour being passed through a unique copper Berry Chamber that dates to the 1920s. Botanicals are arranged there on four trays and slowly infused in the vapour before being condensed back to spirit.

This somewhat resembles the Carterhead process, in that it relies on the vapours passing over the key botanicals in order to create the desired flavour. The package is a most attractive one, with much emphasis on the number five: five sides; five Celtic botanicals; a five-pointed asterisk decorating the bottle; and so on. Caorunn thus proudly style themselves a 'small-batch Scottish gin' and bottle at 41.8% abv. Though technically this could be described as London Dry it's a measure of the owner's self-assurance and confidence in the Scottish heritage that this takes pride of place on the packaging.

And why not? Great gin was always made in Scotland and Caorunn proudly uphold that tradition.

20

CHASE ELEGANT

BRAND OWNER:	Williams Chase Distillery Ltd
DISTILLERY:	Chase Distillery, Rosemaund Farm, Hereford
WEBSITE:	www.chasedistillery.co.uk and www.williamschase.co.uk
VISITOR CENTRE:	Yes
STRENGTH:	48%
OTHER VARIANTS:	Great British, Pink Grapefruit, Seville Orange, Sloe & Mulberry

Once upon a time a hard-up Herefordshire potato farmer found there was more money in making premium crisps than selling spuds, and so Tyrell's Crisps were born. Then this entrepreneurial fellow, one William Chase, discovered small-batch potato vodka and found there was more money in making luxury vodka than premium crisps. It also used up the smaller potatoes that weren't suitable for making crisps. Handy, that.

Enter some venture capitalists who paid £30m (some accounts say £40m) for the crisp company, but he soon fell out with them. Still, no longer hard up, that allowed him to acquire a large yacht, a lot of property and a £3m distillery with a seventy-foot-high rectifying column (it's every bit as tall as it sounds; I went to see it and looking up at it made my neck hurt). Now, I don't know about you, but I like a salty snack with my beverages. However, the venture capitalists, by now no longer the best of friends, didn't agree and so the Tyrell name disappeared from the vodka bottles and Chase Distillery emerged.

Fortunately Chase had got in ahead of the rush to small-brand premium vodkas, was well financed and smartly run by an experienced businessman, and made a fine product, so all went well. Jamie Baxter, whose name you will see several times in this book, was the first distiller. Being based on a farm, Chase grows other things such as apples (this is Herefordshire, after all) and they provide the base for the vodka that they turn to gin. This isn't unique (as the name suggests, Tuthilltown's Half Moon Orchard Gin is also apple based), but it is fairly unusual.

A total of 450 litres of the apple-based vodka is then placed in Ginny, a separate copper pot still with a Carterhead vapour chamber where a pillowcase full of botanicals turns the spirit into gin prior to arriving in the small condenser. The botanicals are conventional enough, other than the addition of hops and fresh apples: which seems fitting, as the distillery buildings were once an experimental hop kiln and the National Association of Cider Makers had a trial orchard here.

At the heart of the Chase success is the fact that this is a family-owned, estate-grown and estate-distilled product. It's bottled on site and Chase proudly proclaim it to be 'field to bottle'. Better still, much of the waste goes to feed their herd of pedigree Hereford cattle. The circle is complete!

21

CHELSEA FLOWER

BRAND OWNER: Partridges of Sloane Square Ltd

DISTILLERY: Dunnet Bay Distillers, Thurso, Caithness

WEBSITE: www.partridges.co.uk

VISITOR CENTRE: Yes (London shop); visitor centre at distillery

STRENGTH: 41.5%

OTHER VARIANTS: Chelsea Flower No. 2 (limited edition)

I was reluctant to include many more third-party distilled gins in this new edition, preferring to highlight the many new craft distilleries that have added such colour and variety to our life – but had to make an exception for this one.

Though it's sold exclusively by the rather smart London grocers Partridges (Royal Warrant holders to Her Majesty Queen Elizabeth II no less), they make no secret of the fact that they don't make it. In fact, as they are happy to explain, it's made for them by Martin Murray of Rock Rose fame (see entry 76) as a celebration of their forty-fifth anniversary. The production information is there on the website and all across the back label, so you couldn't get any more transparent than that – something that some other small brands might like to consider.

Murray, they explain, is a highly acclaimed distiller (you read it here first as early as September 2015 when he had just opened up), and they understandably trade on this association. Much is also made of the fact that the distillery is close to the home of the family's great-great-great-grandmother Mary Sinclair. But they've lost me with that one. Try as I might, the relevance of this entirely escapes me. Marketing, I suppose. Regardless of the property link, though, what we have here is a cracking wee drop, but bear in mind that it comes in the smaller half-litre bottle so beloved of the craft scene. Very tastefully presented, however, and though it's nothing at all to do with the Chelsea Flower Show everything comes up smelling of roses when this is served.

Whether Murray has gone mad with the rose petals – one of nineteen botanicals – I couldn't say, but it is a very fresh and floral drop of gin, especially if you follow the serving recommendation and garnish with borage flowers and more rose petals. Apparently it commemorates 'the historic association between flowers and nurseries and the King's Road in Chelsea'.

To be honest, I don't think we need the flowery prose. Look, it's a great-tasting gin made by some of the good guys with a very pretty label from a posh shop. Enough already.

There's also the limited edition Chelsea Flower No. 2 which was created to mark the wedding of a certain royal personage to an actress. Probably all gone by now but it was very nice.

CITADELLE

BRAND OWNER:	Cognac Pierre Ferrand
DISTILLERY:	Ferrand, Ars, France
WEBSITE:	www.citadellegin.com
VISITOR CENTRE:	No
STRENGTH:	44%
OTHER VARIANTS:	Réserve, Old Tom, Wild Blossom

Citadelle is made in France, in the heart of the Cognac region, using direct-fired cognac stills. It was one of the first 'artisanal' distillers to produce gin, releasing the first batch of Citadelle in 1995 and the oak-aged 'yellow gin' Réserve in 2008.

Cognac distillers Ferrand are limited by law to producing brandy between November and March each year, meaning that the stills traditionally lie idle for six months of the year. That seemed a waste to company owner Alexandre Gabriel, so he decided to put his all-too-still stills to use by making gin in the months he could not produce cognac: 'I always loved the extreme complexity and the finesse that gin offered but was frustrated with what the market had to offer, which was usually too sharp for my taste. My dream was to produce gin with a capital "G" – Gin with some importance.'

So he began to study the distillation methods used to make genièvre – the French ancestor of gin. With the help of a scholar he rummaged through a century-old archive in Dunkirk where, amongst the crumbling papers, they found notes on ancient distillation methods to make gin (some as old as 250 years). A five-year battle to get the necessary permissions then ensued, but we can all be glad that M. Gabriel persisted.

Using nineteen different botanicals, infused for seventy-two hours, distilled for twelve hours using a small (twenty-hectolitre) hammered-copper pot still, and then rested before bottling at 44% Citadelle is a product of great subtlety and sophistication. As they explain: 'few gins are produced in pot stills, and Citadelle is the only gin distilled in a cognac pot still with a naked flame. Distilling gin on an open flame requires a deft touch and far more attention than a column still or steam distillation which is otherwise used. It also means the gin is made in smaller batches, one cask at a time allowing the master distiller to precisely discard the "heads" and "tails" of the distillation, and only keeping the precious, flavourful "heart" of the distillation.'

The oak-aged Réserve is particularly worthy of attention. Each annual batch is clearly dated and represents an evolution of the house style. It's a product made with great care, love and experience, reflected in a complex and rewarding taste that continues to satisfy and evolve to the bottom of the glass. Sipped neat it is a revelation.

23

CITY OF LONDON

BRAND OWNER:	City of London Distillery Ltd
DISTILLERY:	COLD Bar, 22–24 Bride Lane, London
WEBSITE:	www.cityoflondondistillery.com
VISITOR CENTRE:	Bar
STRENGTH:	41.3%
OTHER VARIANTS:	Christopher Wren, Old Tom, Square Mile, Sloe

At the height of the Gin Craze (1720–1751) it has been estimated that in parts of London one house in every four was a gin shop; this in addition to the countless hawkers selling gin on the street. In 1729, when the first Gin Act was passed, there were some 1,500 recorded distillers in London alone and, we may safely presume, any number of entirely clandestine operations.

So our ancestors would not have been remotely surprised to step into a pub and find a distillery there. That essentially describes the City of London Distillery, which is located in the COLD Bar on Bride Lane, just off Fleet Street. Stepping down to the basement bar comes as a total revelation to today's drinker. On the one hand is the splendidly stocked bar, complete with period décor and gin ephemera, and directly opposite, behind a plate-glass window, are the stills, nicknamed Jennifer and Clarissa.

They were first operational in December 2012, under the watchful eye of distiller Jamie Baxter (formerly of Chase Distillery and now masterminding Burleigh's operations, when not consulting for eager new craft distillers). Distilling and bottling of COLD gin takes place here, making the bar a curiosity in its own right as the only manufacturing business in the City of London. I'm told that, as such, it attracts banking and finance types who creatively expense their visit as 'research into manufacturing industry'!

The bar itself has been through several incarnations. As a bright and ambitious young graduate my first place of employment was not far from Bride Lane. I wondered aloud one day why the company's senior directors frequently retired at lunchtime and returned late in the afternoon rather 'tired and emotional'. In tones that brooked no further enquiry I was told that they had 'been to a meeting' at the City Golf Club – in actual fact, the self-same licensed premises that today house the COLD distillery. Had it been there then I doubt they would ever have returned to their desks.

The gin itself is now available at some retailers and in other smart bars. It's a clean, crisp spirit with a pronounced citrus note – very tasty! At the COLD Bar you can take a tasting tour, make your own personal bottle in their trial still, or even commission 200 bottles of your own bespoke creation – a contemporary twist on an important part of London's gin heritage.

24

CONKER

BRAND OWNER: Conker Spirit Ltd

DISTILLERY: Conker, Unit 3, 16A Inverleigh Road, Southbourne, Dorset

WEBSITE: www.conkerspirit.co.uk

VISITOR CENTRE: No

STRENGTH: 40%

OTHER VARIANTS: None

Here's another one. Another bold pioneer prepared to abandon their chosen career, give up all those hopes and dreams, all those examinations, and chuck it all in to become a distiller. They must be bonkers!

In this case, our hero is former chartered surveyor Rupert Holloway, who in setting up Dorset's first distillery freely acknowledges that 'there's no ancient family recipe or mythical Master Distiller here, just a dogged pursuit of the new and exciting'. That's refreshing.

As he goes on to admit in his engaging blog, he's largely self-taught. Asked how he went from chartered surveyor to Master Distiller (just teasing there, Rupert) he says 'Anything can be learnt. So it appears that a lack of knowledge is no longer a barrier to entry. Pick any subject – no matter how complex or obscure – and you'll find everything you need from your phone. Today, your ability to become the expert in the room on practically any subject is restricted only by your tenacity to learn it (and perhaps your phone's battery life)'

It only took forty-five recipe trials, though they went back to number thirty-eight after all that. Tenacity, you see. But in a little over four years, Conker has gone from strength to strength, and is starting to think about expansion while collecting some notable awards for their Dorset Dry gin. Dorset because of the fruity and herbaceous notes from the Dorset-inspired botanicals of elderberries, marsh samphire and handpicked gorse flowers. No horse chestnuts in there, though, which I'll admit did slightly surprise me given the name (they do make an occasional appearance elsewhere as a botanical).

However, I can't argue with the product. What we have here is good value for the small-batch distilling scene (about £35 for a full 70cl bottle) and it's bright and fresh without departing too far from a properly balanced juniper heart. The packaging stands out, too, as distinctive, with its cheery emphasis on Conker's 'That's the Spirit' line.

All in all, this comes across as honest and to the point. There is a commendable directness and transparency to the proposition, reflected in some soul-baring by Rupert on his blog – though, to be critical for a moment, it could do with a few more recent entries. Still, I expect he's busy: this is Rupert the Conqueror, after all, and as he now knows, gin distilling for the self-employed is far from the nine-to-five life of the chartered surveyor!

25

COTSWOLDS

BRAND OWNER: Cotswolds Distillery Company

DISTILLERY: Cotswolds Distillery, Stourton, Shipston-on-Stour

WEBSITE: www.cotswoldsdistillery.com

VISITOR CENTRE: Yes

STRENGTH: 46%

OTHER VARIANTS: Hedgerow, 1616 Barrel Aged

If you look hard enough you'll find two 'Cotswold Gins' out there. Confusing, isn't it? Well, this one is actually distilled in the heart of the Cotswolds in a rather lovely distillery in a charmingly bucolic setting.

The operation was established by former financier Daniel Szor. (Who says something good can't become of such people? Would that all bankers took up some small craft industry and got their hands dirty.) He saw the light some years ago, abandoned the City and followed his dream of making whisky in the Cotswolds with locally grown and malted barley. Good idea, but tough on the cash flow.

So, using a bespoke top-quality German still, Cotswolds added gin to their line-up – and very good it is too. Perhaps that's not surprising: they have actually gone to the lengths of employing a botanist to advise on local botanicals, and they aim to grow many of the rarer botanicals on site (I told you it was charming).

The distinctive, non-standard botanicals include Cotswolds lavender and bay leaf, grapefruit and lime which are contained in a Carterhead-style basket rather than being macerated and distilled with the base spirit. The finished product is not chill filtered. This may result in a slight cloudiness when ice is added but contributes to a smooth and rounded mouthfeel, which goes very well alongside the citrus and pine-juniper notes which are very much to the fore here.

It's a product that works well in a conventional G&T but is also a fine cocktail base. The distillery themselves suggest the Corpse Reviver No. 2. That's a splendid libation which, in the words of the immortal Harry Craddock, is 'to be taken before 11 a.m., or whenever steam and energy are needed'. But don't forget his cautionary note: 'Four of these taken in swift succession will quickly unrevive the corpse again.'

The level of investment here – on distillery, offices and visitor centre, packaging, not to mention the youthful and enthusiastic team – speaks of a deep and lasting investment by Szor who claims not to have an 'exit strategy' (you might imagine at first glance that a call from a big distiller is hoped for, but I genuinely believe this isn't the case). It's illustrative of the fact that the 'craft distilling' sector is growing up very fast and, in its better exponents, more than capable of producing distinctive and interesting products that add variety to our drinking repertoire.

26

CUCUMBER

BRAND OWNER: The English Drinks Company

DISTILLERY: The Langley Distillery, Langley
Green, Warley, West Midlands

WEBSITE: www.englishdrinkscompany.co.uk

VISITOR CENTRE: No

STRENGTH: 40%

OTHER VARIANTS: Classic Pink

Oh dear. 'It has been a common saying of physicians in England that a cucumber should be well sliced, and dressed with pepper and vinegar, and then thrown out, as good for nothing.' So said the Sage of Lichfield, the great Dr Samuel Johnson himself. But was he right?

A cucumber-flavoured gin isn't exactly a new or ground-breaking idea. After all, Hendrick's was launched as long ago as 1999 (positively an eternity in gin years); Martin Miller's hints at it; Canada's Long Table Distillery offers us its take using cucumbers from British Columbia; and even good old Gordon's has raided the corporate cold frames to bring us their Crisp Cucumber.

What's more, there is no English Drinks Company distillery; like many others, they turn to a contract distiller to produce the liquid and concentrate their time and effort on actually selling the stuff. The thing is, though, it's actually rather good, and if what you're good at is sales and marketing, there is some sense in getting experts to make the product.

You do have to like cucumber, because this is very cucumber-y. It reminds me of summer, of cricket teas, of lazy picnics by a meandering river – the essence of cucumber leaps from the bottle and demands to be finely sliced and placed, with infinite care, between two delicate, almost transparent slices of crustless white bread, lightly buttered and eaten with an insouciant air. Yes, this is a very cucumber-y gin and your reaction to it will depend entirely upon your view of this humble comestible. After the cucumber there are some peppery notes and a bit of a juniper bite, but cucumber is the big star here and doesn't let you forget it.

But it is not to be underrated: the remarkable cucumber is noted for its contribution to healthy skin, relief from constipation, diabetes, kidney problems, acidity, sunburn and as an antidote to bad breath. Pliny knew it to be a generally good thing.

Anyway, gin and cucumber has a long, if not illustrious, literary history. The unforgettable Sarah Gamp, the disreputable nurse of Dickens' *Martin Chuzzlewit*, loved them: 'In case there should be such a thing as a cowcumber in the 'ouse, will you be so kind as bring it, for I'm rather partial to 'em, and they does a world of good in a sick room.'

Whether or not it works in gin I couldn't possibly say, but it must be worth trying.

DARNLEY'S VIEW

BRAND OWNER: Wemyss Malts Ltd

DISTILLERY: Darnley's, Kingsbarns, St Andrews, Fife

WEBSITE: www.darnleysgin.com

VISITOR CENTRE: Yes

STRENGTH: 40%

OTHER VARIANTS: Spiced, Navy Strength

In my line of work I'm exposed to a fair old amount of PR and marketing guff. The theory goes that brands have to have a back story, some sort of heritage or provenance that will provide emotional engagement for the consumer. There's a whole industry of 'brand consultants' driving BMWs on the strength of this stuff.

Most of the time, when it bears some sort of more or less oblique relationship to the truth, it's harmless enough and sometimes it actually tells us something important or relevant about the product. Occasionally though the spinmeisters get carried away. Consider the following about Darnley's View (launched 2010).

> Scotland, 1565. Mary Queen of Scots first spies her future husband, Lord Darnley, through the courtyard window of Wemyss Castle, the historic family seat of renowned vintners and spirits merchants, the Wemyss family (pronounced 'weems'). Today, in recognition of this defining moment, they bring you the superbly balanced, hand crafted Darnley's View Gin.

In its way, it's a little masterpiece – the skilful introduction of an entirely spurious heritage and cast of historical characters, with little more than merely corroborative detail, intended to give artistic verisimilitude to an otherwise bald and unconvincing narrative. (See how I worked Poo-Bah's words from W. S. Gilbert's *Mikado* in there? It has nothing whatsoever to do with gin but gives a sort of cultural gloss to my text – that's how the trick works.)

I could go on, but the question that remains is why they bother. This is a perfectly drinkable, well-made London Dry gin, originally sourced from the highly regarded Thames Distillers but now produced in their own distillery just outside St Andrews. It's nicely packaged, tastes good and is great value for money. The companion Spiced Gin is laced with cinnamon and nutmeg, proving an exceptionally fine drop.

Especially now that it's distilled in Scotland, I'd be happier to see this promoted on its own merits, rather than on the back of some elaborately contrived story that really can't hold water. Wemyss have a great reputation for their single cask malt whisky; and with their excellent credentials I'd like to see them selling Darnley's View as the cracking, great-value, easy-drinking and thoroughly agreeable product that it is and leave the long-dead aristos out of it.

DIPLÔME

BRAND OWNER:	BeBo Drinks
DISTILLERY:	Boudier, Dijon, France
WEBSITE:	www.diplomedrygin.com
VISITOR CENTRE:	No
STRENGTH:	44%
OTHER VARIANTS:	None

$\mathcal{D}id$ you know that the famous French scientist Professor Louis Pasteur started investigating the action of yeast on fermentation in a sugar-beet distillery in Lille in 1856? His work transformed the brewing and distilling industry and is the basis of everything that we know today about fermentation (basically for present purposes, turning a sugar solution into alcohol).

I mention this because the spirit base for Diplôme is made from beetroot (I assume sugar beet). That may sound odd, but in fact if something contains sugar you can ferment it, and a wide variety of sugars are found throughout nature. The yields will vary, of course, as will the flavour, but the end result will be a low-strength alcohol that can be distilled. Not many distillers today use a sugar beet base but then, as the French say, *chacun à son goût*.

I do not idly introduce this Gallic connection, for Diplôme is made in France – I note for your curiosity that neither the brand website nor the UK importer discloses the identity of the distiller, other than to say it is in Dijon. That is powerfully suggestive of Boudier, proprietors of their own Saffron gin and contract distiller of Hoxton, but, as no one will say definitively, this remains a speculation. I have no idea why they would wish to be so secretive, but there it is. I'm going to say Boudier until someone contradicts me.

What we are permitted to know is that the juniper berries, coriander, whole lemons, orange peel, angelica, saffron, iris root and fennel seed are infused in the spirit before being distilled in a pot still and eventually bottled at 44%. A fairly straightforward and old-school selection, then, with the notable exception of saffron, which again points to a circumstantial connection with Boudier. The simplicity of the recipe reflects the fact that this dates to the Second World War, when Diplôme was apparently the gin of choice of the US forces in Europe, hence the reference on the rather charming, typographically rich label (curiously similar to the Boudier house style) to the 'Original 1945 Recipe'.

Diplôme seems to have faded after the war and disappeared from the scene entirely until resurrected on the back of the current wave of enthusiasm for gins with authentic histories. It was relaunched as recently as 2013 but apparently already enjoys widespread worldwide distribution.

Beyond this, what I do not know I cannot tell. *C'est un mystère extraordinaire.*

29

DISTILLERIE DE PARIS

BRAND OWNER: La Distillerie de Paris

DISTILLERY: La Distillerie de Paris, 54 Passage Reilhac, 75010 Paris

WEBSITE: http://www.distillerie.paris/

VISITOR CENTRE: No

STRENGTH: 43%

OTHER VARIANTS: Gin Tonik, Bel Air

It's hard to convey the excitement surrounding this tiny distillery. Remarkably, it's the first to be built in Paris for more than a century and the carefully crafted, almost spiritual approach that has been adopted by founders Nicolas and Sébastien Julhès has captured the imagination of France's cutting-edge spirits lovers. Even more remarkably, it only began operations in earnest in January 2015 but has already established an enviable reputation.

Working first from their family-run gourmet delicatessen, and with experience in product and brand consultancy for leading drinks companies, it still required five years of work, planning and negotiations to get the necessary permits to open their distillery. But with that background and with exposure to the booming world of craft spirits, the brothers have been able to bring both relevant experience and a worldview to their project.

They do not make only gin. From their 400-litre Holstein still they are also creating vodka and rum and a malt spirit which will, given time, become Paris's first-ever whisky. While they are anything but cheap (expect to pay the standard bottle equivalent of more than £60), these are truly exceptional products, made with great love and attention, flair and a complete conviction of spirit by true and deeply committed enthusiasts. Think of their gin as an artwork, or as the bespoke creation of a great perfumier or chef at the height of their powers and you will understand and appreciate these products. They come from the heart but with an underlying philosophical and intellectual conviction.

So, I am going to come right out and say it: I found these amongst the most exciting, interesting and engaging spirits that I tasted for this book. That is remarkable enough; it is nothing short of astonishing that they have come from a distillery a little over three years old, hidden away in a courtyard in the heart of Paris (it's less than five minutes from the Gare du Nord). While I was aware of the buzz surrounding the distillery, nothing prepared me for the quality and verve of these products.

As you will see from some of the other entries, I am seduced by gins with a citrus note. Here bergamot and jasmine merge wonderfully well with the juniper notes, creating a spirit that intrigues and delights in equal measure. I do not know what the future holds for La Distillerie but I am sure that it will prosper. *Fluctuat nec mergitur.*

30

DOCKYARD

BRAND OWNER: Russell Distillers Ltd

DISTILLERY: Copper Rivet Distillery, Chatham

WEBSITE: www.copperrivetdistillery.com

VISITOR CENTRE: Yes

STRENGTH: 41.2%

OTHER VARIANTS: None

Here we see the craft distilling movement getting serious and really upping its game with a significant investment in premises, equipment and product development. The distillery is based in the magnificent Victorian Pump House No. 5 in the historic Chatham Dockyard, and located on the splendidly named Leviathan Way, where it has breathed new life into buildings which were abandoned in the mid-1980s when the dockyards were closed – something of an economic and emotional disaster for Chatham and the Medway.

Owned by the Russell family, who have links to the retail side of the drinks industry, Copper Rivet aims to reflect the engineering, innovation and entrepreneurship that once characterised this location. So, as well as refurbishing the impressive building (which they bought), they have worked with Master Distiller Abhi Banik, once of the prestigious Heriot-Watt International Centre of Brewing and Distilling in Edinburgh, to design their own unique gin still. Now that's bold – virtually everyone buys their stills from one of the established makers.

Just to add to the frisson of uncertainty that must have accompanied that decision, they didn't take their design to a recognised stillmaker to have it built. They turned instead to a local business to fabricate this and their own mighty column still where they make their high-strength neutral grain base. Fortunately, it's all turned out very well: not only did this underpin their local credentials but the still – romantically named Joyce – makes cracking gin.

It's their own exclusive recipe, naturally, developed after an exhaustive series of trials and consumer tests and, unusually, based on complete control of the entire process from grain to glass. Now that is painstaking and the sign of some true obsessives.

Dockyard gin is dry to taste, with an old-fashioned juniper and citrus note that will appeal to discriminating gin purists looking for complexity and great balance. All this is complemented by the slightly higher than normal strength and a striking presentation though I'd personally like to see a 70cl bottle being offered, having witnessed my neighbours polish off the contents of the current 50cl packaging before I could pour my own G&T.

'The Dockyard Spirit Endures' they say on the side of the bottle – well, not round here it didn't, but everything seems pleasingly shipshape at Copper Rivet.

31

DODD'S

BRAND OWNER:	The London Distillery Company Ltd
DISTILLERY:	London Distillery, 58 Druid Street, Bermondsey, London
WEBSITE:	www.londondistillery.com
VISITOR CENTRE:	By appointment
STRENGTH:	49.9%
OTHER VARIANTS:	Old Tom, Kew Organic, Organic Explorer's Strength, Kew Orangery

Poor old Ralph Dodd. This would-be entrepreneur, having failed in his dream to bore a tunnel under the River Thames, determined to start a distillery. Unfortunately, he omitted to complete the no doubt tedious legal formalities, was challenged by rivals and in 1807 was obliged to drop his scheme without a drop ever being distilled. He died a ruined man.

You might think him more deserving of a Darwin Award than having a splendid new gin named after him. But, perverse or not, that's what the folks at the London Distillery Company (LDC) elected to do and, in his honour, they've created a splendidly packaged gin with lots of engineering references on the label – and, I'm happy to say, a very fine product to which I'm sure old Ralph would have been happy to lend his name.

The company was created to be the first distiller of whisky in London since 1903 and has been busy making drams since raising the funds it needed from a combination of equity financing and a clever use of crowd-funding. But you have to wait for whisky, and anyway we're interested in the gin, which is available right now.

In a market now crowded by craft distillers, LDC does stand out for its obsessive approach to its product. Using its own proprietary method (not dissimilar to what Hendrick's does on a much larger scale), a base spirit is distilled in Christina, a 140-litre copper pot still. The organic ingredients, which are approved by the Soil Association, include juniper, angelica, fresh lime peel, and honey from London hives. Now that's unusual, but you really can taste the difference that it makes.

A small proportion of the base is then used to macerate more delicate botanicals such as bay laurel, cardamom and red raspberry leaf for twenty-four hours. This is then distilled for a second time in Little Albion, a rotary evaporator (cold vacuum still). The two spirits are married for several weeks before being hand-bottled at 49.9% abv and labelled at the distillery in batches of 100 to 500 bottles.

The brand's responsible drinking message (they had to have one, I suppose) is taken from Ralph Dodd's prospectus for the launch of his ill-fated distillery business: *'It is an evil too well known to require a dissertation – for the consequence arising from bad spirits, soon manifests in the destruction of its user.'*

And so say all of us!

32

EDINBURGH GIN

BRAND OWNER:	Ian Macleod Distillers Ltd.
DISTILLERY:	The Edinburgh Gin Distillery, 1a Rutland Place, Edinburgh
WEBSITE:	www.edinburghgindistillery.co.uk
VISITOR CENTRE:	Within Heads & Tails Bar
STRENGTH:	43%
OTHER VARIANTS:	Seaside, Cannonball, Valentine's, Christmas, 1670

Edinburgh Gin – it's made in Edinburgh in case you were wondering – could be held up as a case study for the craft distilling movement. It was the brainchild of Alex and Jane Nicol who are the husband and wife team behind Sheep Dip and other super whiskies. But Alex is a restless sort of chap and possessed of a fierce entrepreneurial drive – so much so that he's recently been able to sell the brand to his distributors Ian Macleod Distillers (and can now afford to buy me a drink).

Back in 2010, observing the growing interest in gin, he determined to launch his own. But the entrepreneur in him has a streak of caution so rather than immediately open a small distillery he had others make it for him. However, before long, sales grew to the point where a distillery could be considered. Once, Edinburgh had a flourishing distilling industry producing both gin and whisky – one eighteenth-century text claims that the city was home to more than 400 illicit stills, but that owes rather more to the overheated imagination of the partisan author (a fervent abolitionist) than any verifiable fact. Gin distilling died out in Edinburgh when the Melrose-Drover gin distillery in Leith closed in 1974.

The Nicols re-established the tradition with a pub distillery at one end of Princes Street in a cosy basement bar, where you can see Flora and Caledonia behind glass and book educational tours and tastings. It's so much more fun than the light industrial units that are home to some other small-batch producers though, truth to tell, they have another larger unit in Leith.

The distillery is constantly experimenting with flavoured expressions and has recently launched a navy strength version; first produced in the shadow of Edinburgh Castle it's been named Cannonball. As the name would suggest, it's explosive stuff!

There's also a handsomely packaged collaboration with Edinburgh's world-famous Royal Botanic Garden, called 1670 – a homage to the original physic garden created by two pioneering Edinburgh doctors. The result is a contemporary gin that is rooted in a fascinating chapter of Edinburgh's history.

The Nicols' business has evolved to the point where their own distillery was the logical next stage in their development and a trade sale perhaps inevitable. With Edinburgh Gin they lent interest, variety and colour to this most respectable and middle-class of cities: lang may their lum reek!

33

ELEPHANT

BRAND OWNER:	Elephant Gin Ltd
DISTILLERY:	Schwechower, nr Hamburg, Germany
WEBSITE:	www.elephant-gin.com
VISITOR CENTRE:	No
STRENGTH:	45%
OTHER VARIANTS:	Elephant Strength, Aged Sloe

We all probably remember Babar from childhood; or Kipling's Elephant's Child and his 'satiable curtiosity'; or tales of Jumbo (late of London Zoo) and the great showman P.T. Barnum; or Mark Twain's 'Stolen White Elephant'. These gentle giants exercise a powerful hold on our imagination. Here in the 'civilised' West we deplore the wholesale slaughter of the African elephant to satisfy the apparently insatiable Chinese demand for ivory. Though you're probably feeling vaguely bad about that, few of us (and I'm as guilty as anyone) actually do very much about it.

But now you can! It's easy! Drink Elephant Gin (no elephants harmed in the making)!

Yes, company founder Robin Gerlach and his partners were so troubled by the 35,000 African elephants killed every year that they determined to help. After something of an epiphany on an African bush holiday they hit upon the idea of making Elephant Gin and contributing 15% of its profits to elephant conservation.

Soon Gerlach had to give up his day job in finance (like Daniel Szor, another banker turned gin distiller) to concentrate on sales and marketing. Today, the product is distilled at the rather beautiful Schwechower distillery in Germany, where they make very fine fruit spirits, but the partners are actively looking to set up their own operation, probably using the current still.

I must admit to a certain cynicism, assuming that the elephants were simply a marketing gimmick. I couldn't have been more wrong: while Gerlach can and does speak eloquently about his gin he moves to a different level when talking about elephants.

You probably care more about the unusual botanicals. They include baobab, the extraordinary buchu plant, devil's claw and African wormwood, sourced with the assistance of native African tribespeople. The botanicals also include mountain pine needles, specially cut in the Salzburger Mountains to complement the juniper. It comes in a custom bottle (50cl) with a splendid closure and handsome label – one of the best-dressed craft gins you can buy.

It's not cheap but all things considered it is great value. Please don't forget that!

FARMER'S ORGANIC

BRAND OWNER: Chatham Imports Inc.

DISTILLERY: Undisclosed

WEBSITE: www.farmersgin.com

VISITOR CENTRE: No

STRENGTH: 46.7%

OTHER VARIANTS: None

Another small-batch gin from the United States, Farmer's has the distinction of its organic status, which it announces proudly and prominently on the label. There are a few organic gins out there, but only a few, so if this is important to you you'll have to do some searching. If you really care about such things, bear in mind that this organic certification comes from the USDA and is therefore subtly different from the UK's Soil Association. I'm not saying one is better than the other, just pointing it out.

Now, I'm not entirely convinced of the particular benefits of organic production to spirits. That's not to suggest that there aren't sound environmental and ethical reasons for organic production, it's simply a comment on the taste. But, after some consideration, that view probably comes from the dark spirits perspective, where wood maturation has a significant influence and the original spirit character is less evident. Clearly that's not the case for gin, and here – whether due to organic production or not – we have a clean, fresh and very floral-tasting gin that stands up very well against its peers.

It's helped by the 46.7% abv strength. Not overpowering but with plenty of body, this means Farmer's excels as a cocktail ingredient and is not overwhelmed by even a good slug of tonic. As an example of the 'New American Gin' style the key point in the taste is that juniper has been dialled down (compared to, say, a British classic such as Beefeater), allowing other, arguably more subtle botanicals to come to the fore.

Here we have elderflower and lemongrass that are evident on the palate, contributing to a less assertive but no less complex gin that I would expect to do well in blind tasting.

The owners, Chatham Imports, are a little coy about the distillery, simply saying that it's the same as their Crop Harvest Earth Organic vodka. Sadly, I'm none the wiser, but whoever is distilling Farmer's knows what they're about, so let's hope they keep it up.

The secret lies in the soil, you know.

35

FERDINAND'S

BRAND OWNER: Ferdinand's

DISTILLERY: Avadis, Wincheringen, Germany

WEBSITE: www.saar-gin.com

VISITOR CENTRE: No

STRENGTH: 44%

OTHER VARIANTS: Quince, Goldcap

There seems to be no stopping those wacky Germans trying to reinvent gin. The guys at Ferdinand's aren't happy with using thirty (thirty, count 'em) botanicals and coming up with their own individual distilling regime. Oh no. They then go and add a dollop (well, a precisely measured 2.5% by volume – they are German) of Riesling wine into the spirit prior to bottling. What's going on, you might ask, and can we really admit this as gin?

Well, it's clearly different, and, even if you'd be hard pressed to pick out all thirty botanicals (I certainly was), the initial impact is one of great power, complexity and assurance. There is an initial sweetness, presumably due to the Riesling wine, that is soon washed away by the intense botanical hit, juniper follow-through and gingery finish. It's definitely more than a gimmick or a novelty, and, having met the enthusiastic young production team, I can confirm how seriously they take all this.

Most distillers will tell you that there's a realistic upper limit to the number of botanicals that you need and indeed want in your gin, the fact of the matter being that after a certain point the individual contributions get overwhelmed or even start cancelling each other out. Adding botanicals increases the cost and complexity of the distilling process but doesn't necessarily add flavour or even complexity to the taste. Different botanicals behave differently – some need to be infused in the spirit, while others perform best on a vapour tray. So working with botanicals, particularly unorthodox ones, is a tricky business and needs a confident and skilled hand to manage it well.

But distiller Andreas Vallendar comes from a long and distinguished family line of distillers that have been making fruit schnapps since 1824. His Avadis Distillery is small but expertly set up, and clearly capable of making high-quality spirit (he also makes the highly regarded ThreeLand malt whisky). The Riesling wine that is added is not some supermarket plonk but from the nearby VDP Forstmeister Geltz-Zilliken vineyard, whose top vintages go into Ferdinand's gin.

When I first encountered this I was sceptical. Having tried it, however, I'm completely won over. Naturally, it's not cheap – you'll pay the equivalent of nearly £70 for a standard bottle – but this is a product you'll want to drink thoughtfully and carefully in a well-mixed cocktail.

So, to conclude: it's gin, Jim, but not as we know it. And all the better for that.

36

FISHER'S

BRAND OWNER: Fisher's Gin Ltd

DISTILLERY: Adnams, Copper House Distillery, Southwold, Suffolk

WEBSITE: www.fishersgin.com

VISITOR CENTRE: Yes, for distillery

STRENGTH: 44%

OTHER VARIANTS: None

Here's a gin made in England but with its eyes fixed firmly across the Channel, so I felt it worth including as representative of the many new small-batch products now flooding the French market as our neighbours experience their own gin boom. (But you can get it here as well.)

It's actually distilled by Adnams, who have been distilling their own gins and vodka since 2010 in a substantial purpose-built distillery adjacent to their rather more famous brewery. The entrepreneur behind the Fisher's venture has long-standing connections to the Adnams brewing business and also has interests in champagne, so is no stranger to the world of drinks.

And the first thing to notice is that this is a half-litre bottle, something we have come to associate with the craft sector but something to look out for if you are comparing prices or shopping on a strict budget. Almost always, such packaging means the price per centilitre is higher than in the standard 70cl bottle, but it's only fair to point out that Fisher's has been bottled at 44% rather than the more normal 40%. That means you're buying more alcohol and less water.

It was recently tasted by *Fine Spirits Magazine*, where it received qualified approval. What did they think? One taster concluded: '*Pas du tout désagréable, juste un peu bizarre.*'

That seems a little harsh. His colleague's summary was: '*Un côté austere avec un nez rustique qui cache en fait une bouche complexe et cyclique. Intriguant!*'

Well, I imagine '*intriguant*' will be preferred to '*un peu bizarre*'. I actually saw those reviews before I personally tasted the product, and on first meeting it I had to agree that this is definitely not a run-of-the-mill gin. The aim, if you believe what you read on the back label, has been to evoke the coastline of England, 'where the awe-inspiring power of the sea meets the rugged and fertile shores of the British Isles'. Quite a task for a mere gin you might think.

But Adnams distiller John McCarthy has employed traditional English herbs such as spignal and bog myrtle, and the result for me is an elusive sweet spiciness that rather defies description. It grows on you, and so I'm happy to encourage you to try this product of *la perfide Albion* before all the bottles leave our shores!

37

FOUR PILLARS

BRAND OWNER: Healesville Distilling Company
Pty Ltd

DISTILLERY: Four Pillars, South Warrandyte,
Victoria, Australia

WEBSITE: www.fourpillarsgin.com

VISITOR CENTRE: By arrangement

STRENGTH: 41.8%

OTHER VARIANTS: Spiced Negroni, Modern Australian,
Navy Strength, Barrel Aged,
Christmas

As you probably know, the Australians make some great wines in the Yarra. I can still recall a bottle of Yarra Yering Dry Red Wine No. 2 (prosaic title, stunning wine) that has me licking my lips at the memory. So I jump to the assumption that they can probably manage to get something drinkable out of a still.

There is a vibrant craft industry producing whisky, mainly in Tasmania, that has surprised a few folks, and some jolly decent gins are to be found down under as well. One of the newest but most exciting is Four Pillars, also located in the Yarra Valley, not so very far away from Melbourne where the rival Melbourne Gin Company have based their operations. But there appears to be plenty of domestic support, and with growing international interest in these craft gins there is no reason why they can't both prosper.

Four Pillars ran a highly successful crowd-funding campaign that meant their first release sold out before it was made. An impressive £15,500 was raised – quite something for a product that at that point didn't exist and evidence of enthusiastic local backing that gives the brand a vocal and financially committed supporter base. However, they are far from limited in their horizons and ambitions, with a stated aim 'to make the best craft spirits in Australia'. That is already a demanding goal and will only get harder. So what are they all about?

The heart of the operation is the first new Christian Carl still in Australia, which they named Wilma, after head distiller Cameron Mackenzie's late mother. Mackenzie comes from a wine background, believes strongly in the use of fresh fruit (he's not alone in this, but it is unusual) and having taken close to eighteen months to come up with the final gin is using some unorthodox botanicals such as lemon myrtle and Tasmanian pepperberry leaf. He also posts an amusing blog on the distillery's website.

Looking into the distillery more closely, I was reminded of The Macallan single malt whisky and their 'six pillars'. Guess how many Four Pillars work with? That's right, just four. One, their copper pot still. Two, the triple-filtered Yarra Valley water. Three, the botanicals: added to the pepperberry, lemon myrtle and fresh oranges we find cinnamon, cardamom, coriander seeds, lavender and star anise and the classic juniper and angelica root. Four, the distillers love what they do and love what they have made. Fair dinkum, mate!

38

GARDEN SWIFT

BRAND OWNER: Capreolus Distillery Ltd

DISTILLERY: Capreolus, The Mount, Park View, Stratton, Cirencester

WEBSITE: www.capreolusdistillery.co.uk

VISITOR CENTRE: No

STRENGTH: 47%

OTHER VARIANTS: Mulberry Barrel Aged

I'm not really sure that 'gin' does this justice and, having discovered Garden Swift (formerly Garden Tiger), I'm far from certain that I want to reveal much about it. My baser instincts tell me to keep this to myself, sharing a tiny glass with trusted friends but only pouring from an unmarked bottle in case they track down their own supply and leave less for me.

Yes, it really is that good. Unfortunately for me, the Whisky Exchange got there first and made this their 'Spirit of the Year' for 2017 (incidentally, Nikka's Coffey Gin – see entry 66 – took the crown for 2018, so that's two gins in a row on a leading whisky retailer website, which tells you something about the current gin boom).

This is an incredible accolade. Capreolus had only been in operation for five months when selected. Out of all the spirits in the world – and some pretty stunning products had been chosen in previous years – a tiny Cotswolds distillery run by a remarkably single-minded individual, wildlife photographer turned distiller Barney Wilczak, came out on top.

Swift or Tiger, this is a truly exceptional product, the result of an obsessive attention to detail: the glass is highly UV-resistant (top tip: dark glass bottles are better for your gin and often indicate a product made with especial care); the corks are very tactile; and the labels – letterpress-printed, naturally – are small works of art.

All this tender loving care heightens your expectations of the product, and you will not be disappointed. Wilczak has gone to immense pains in creating this elixir, an extraordinarily complex and satisfying spirit that will make you rethink everything you thought you knew about gin and how you drink it. This is not just a London Dry but, as Wilczak explains, 'a very complex but integrated spirit that shares the intricacy . . . in eaux de vie'.

With thirty-four botanicals – a combination of home-grown, wild and traded – this is probably the most multifaceted gin currently distilled in the UK, but it would be a mistake to focus on the absolute number, the result of a vast amount of detailed testing and rigorous selection. I could go on, but suggest you visit the website to get the full story.

You can serve this as a G&T or the recommended Chamois cocktail but personally I sip it very slowly, neat and unchilled from a tiny Georgian gin glass, reflecting on the love that has gone into making it.

39

GENEROUS

BRAND OWNER: Ô de Vie S.A.S.

DISTILLERY: 12 Rue Robinière, 16110 La
Rochefoucauld, Cognac, France

WEBSITE: www.generousgin.com

VISITOR CENTRE: No

STRENGTH: 44%

OTHER VARIANTS: None

The fantastically attractive-looking bottle had me seduced even before I broke the seal. This, I prophesy, will be one of the future successes of the craft distilling movement, with the potential for significant growth – provided, of course, that they can manage the necessary increase in production while maintaining quality.

That's not easy. The challenges facing a small company in gearing up production to meet demand are significant. Finding the right people can be difficult, not to mention financing the growth itself.

But that's all in the future. Right now, it's time to enjoy a superbly produced gin from France that looks, feels and tastes like a potential world-beater. The company is small, relatively new and little-known. But from their base in the Cognac region they have been producing two rums (Arcane and Beach House Spiced, if you want to try) and have timed their entry into the gin market very well indeed.

I have to mention the packaging again. It's white glass with a beautiful tree-of-life design fired into the surface of the bottle. The shape fits wonderfully well into your hand and it's immensely satisfying just to handle and cradle the bottle before pouring. I suspect very few of these will end up in the recycling; they'll stay as decoration or be repurposed into lamp stands or even as vases for dried flowers. They're simply too attractive to throw away.

The attention to detail in the packaging alerts you to the fact that this is going to be something special, and the gin itself does not disappoint. I believe any gin distiller anywhere in the world would be proud of this. It's a 44% abv spirit so has a rich, zesty mouthfeel and a long-lasting consistent finish. Generous by name and generous in its nature, there is a lot to savour here. I loved the citrus notes, balanced by floral aromas but with plenty of underlying juniper to endorse the gin credentials and please the purist.

If you sip it neat you'll pick out elderflower (always a great component in gin) and jasmine, but this works superbly well in a classic gin and tonic. You could try alternative garnishes such as grapefruit, satsuma or tangerine to draw out the citrus hints or go floral with a sprig of rosemary or some crushed elderflower leaves.

Just experiment. There are some great gins coming out of Cognac right now and Generous has really set a very high standard for their neighbours.

40

GIN MARE

BRAND OWNER: Giró Ribot & Global Premium
Brands, SA

DISTILLERY: Destilerías Miquel Guansé,
Vilanova i la Geltrú, Spain

WEBSITE: www.ginmare.com

VISITOR CENTRE: No

STRENGTH: 42.7%

OTHER VARIANTS: None

Mundus appellatur caelum, terra et mare', the Latin for 'the world is called heaven, earth and sea' (possibly a reference to the work of the seventh-century saint Isidore, Archbishop of Seville, whose collection of ancient texts greatly influenced the late medieval church), is to be found on a stained-glass window in a former chapel in the little seaside town of Vilanova i la Geltrú on Spain's Costa Gourada. So what, you may ask.

It also appears on the rather striking bottle of Gin Mare – Sea Gin – which today is made in said former chapel. Imagine, a chapel dedicated to gin with the still placed dramatically where the altar once stood: truly they take their gin with an almost religious devotion in Spain.

Since its launch in 2008 Gin Mare, soaked in all the influences of its Mediterranean home, has proved highly successful on the cocktail scene, though when partnered with its stablemate 1724 tonic, it also makes a stunning G&T – especially when served in the generous Spanish style. It is the creation of Marc and Manuel Giró, the fourth generation of a noted Spanish distilling house that is behind the popular GinMG and other brands. Their goal was to create a new contemporary, premium gin that reflected its origins.

To develop it, they exhaustively tested forty-five different botanicals, finally settling on a range that, along with wild juniper harvested from the family estate, included Arbequina olives (small, low yielding and expensive), sweet and bitter oranges and lemons (all painstakingly hand-peeled), rosemary, thyme and basil, and more commonly seen gin botanicals such as coriander and cardamom. Hard though it is to credit, the fruit zests are macerated in neutral spirit for fully twelve months before it is deemed ready for distillation to begin.

That takes place in the distillery's custom-designed 250-litre Florentine pot still (interestingly a similar design is used in perfume manufacture and at G'Vine), after which the finished product is bottled, literally next door to the distillery, at 42.7%.

As might be expected from the unorthodox use of olives, rosemary and so on, this is a different-tasting gin – and one that once tasted won't be forgotten. Understandably, it's not the cheapest gin on the market but, with its unusual make-up and distinctive presentation, still offers excellent value.

If this is the sea, don't hesitate to dive right in.

41

GORDON'S ORIGINAL SPECIAL DRY

BRAND OWNER:	Diageo plc
DISTILLERY:	Cameronbridge, Fife
WEBSITE:	www.gordons-gin.co.uk
VISITOR CENTRE:	No
STRENGTH:	37.5%
OTHER VARIANTS:	Export Strength, Premium Pink, Cucumber, Elderflower, Sloe

If you don't ask for the gin you really want, this is the gin you'll probably get. It really is everywhere. I suppose if you add enough ice and tonic of your choice there's nothing at all wrong with it; indeed traditionalists will enjoy the strong juniper influence. But there's not that much to get terribly excited about either.

Frankly, this was how gin lost its way, became dull, staid and boring, and surrendered to vodka and light rum. When, in 1992, the UK version was reduced to 37.5% abv you really did feel they had run up the white flag, chucked in the towel and given up the ghost. In fairness, the Original London Dry version (mainly duty free shops) is a healthier 47.3% abv, which makes all the difference, but for the classic London gin to drop to the level of an anaemic supermarket own-brand really was disappointing. Gordon's may as well have told us to BOGOF.

After nearly 225 years of history I imagine that founder Alexander Gordon was less than impressed that some bean counter determined the future of his creation, a global English icon if ever there was one, to be a corporate cash cow. Because, make no mistake, less than thirty years ago the prevailing industry view was that gin was finished and it was only a matter of time before it joined shrub, malmsey and other forgotten old favourites in the great off-licence in the sky.

Slowly but surely most of the distinctive Gordon's variants – Old Tom, Orange, and Lemon – were killed off, and though their Sloe gin staggered on, it was hard to find. But it's amazing what a bit of competition can do: enter Bombay Sapphire and, a little later, Hendrick's from William Grant & Sons. From a standing start these two ripped up the rule book: gin wasn't fuddy-duddy, in decline and only to be sold on price. With clever marketing and great products, they proved that you could sell a premium gin to younger drinkers with a funky image – and, what was important, lots and lots of it.

Hendrick's in particular rethought what gin meant and, though they might not see it quite this way, the Gordon's people have a lot to thank them for. Now we can enjoy Gordon's Crisp Cucumber (whatever gave them that idea?), Premium Pink, the subtly sweet Elderflower, and Sloe.

It feels a little bit like Dad dancing to be honest, but bless them for trying. Mr Gordon's legacy may be safe after all.

42

GRANIT

BRAND OWNER:	Alte Hausbrennerei Penninger GmbH
DISTILLERY:	Alte Hausbrennerei Penninger, Hauzenberg, Bavaria, Germany
WEBSITE:	www.granit-gin.com
VISITOR CENTRE:	Schnapps Museum
STRENGTH:	42%
OTHER VARIANTS:	None

Here's a little-known gin from Bavaria – well, I'll admit that I knew nothing at all about it until I was judging the World Gin Awards one year. What happens at this particular stage is that judges are sent lots of little sample bottles labelled only with a code number and the strength, a scoring sheet with the code and instructions on the criteria to apply. I faithfully worked my way through a large box of gins – some good, some not so great – duly scored them and sent off my responses.

Some time later my curiosity could not be contained and when all the scores were in and counted I asked the organisers to identify the one gin that I had scored the highest. And Granit it was, and to my frustration I knew nothing at all about it, except that I obviously liked it very much. And it seems that my fellow judges agreed because this has since picked up some notable wins in the World Gin Awards and also a silver gong from the IWSC.

I described it thus: 'Very attractive nose. Clove, vanilla, nutmeg and pine-y juniper. Well balanced and complex.' They don't give you much room for comments, but this was high praise. So, once I had the identity I had to check this out.

It's made by the old-established family firm of Penninger, who describe themselves as the leading distiller of traditional Bavarian speciality spirits. Granit is a relatively new product, the creation of Stefan Penninger, the latest generation of the family to head the company. He has chosen to employ native Bavarian forest plants and combine them with a highly unusual maturation process. Granit's twenty-eight botanicals include classic gin spices and herbs such as lemon, coriander and cardamom combined with the local melissa, baldmoney (similar to lovage) and gentian root.

Once distilled, the gin is matured for several months in traditional earthenware vats before being filtered through locally hand-cut granite stones of varying sizes using the so-called 'Oxy-Esterator', a fifty-year-old technology which had pride of place in their Penninger Bavarian Schnapps Museum. Hence the name Granit and hence the small granite stone attached to the bottle. This can be placed in the freezer and then used as an ice cube to prevent your drink from becoming watered down. It's also, according to the distillery at least, guaranteed to be a conversation starter! Bottled at 42% Granit is claimed to be 100% organic.

43

GRAVENEY

BRAND OWNER: Graveney Gin Ltd
DISTILLERY: Graveney, Unit 17 Merton Abbey
Mills, Watermill Way, London
WEBSITE: www.graveneygin.co.uk
VISITOR CENTRE: Yes (at 22a Tooting Market)
STRENGTH: 45%
OTHER VARIANTS: None

Could Tooting really be one of 'the world's coolest neighbourhoods'? Does it rank alongside the hipster hangouts of Brooklyn, Seattle and Rio? Well, *Lonely Planet* thinks so, rating Tooting 'uber-cool' for its gritty charm, multiculturalism and originality. I don't believe it was tongue-in-cheek or even the slightest facetious, so what's going on?

Well, Graveney Gin for one thing. Taking its name from the local River Graveney, a less than mighty tributary of the Wandle, the distillery started, almost by accident, when former banker Victoria Christie was overwhelmed by local support at the Tootopia festival in September 2015. Having painstakingly made 200 bottles, six at a time, virtually all sold out in one frenzied weekend and, faced with cries of 'More!', a swift crowd-funding campaign enabled her to create a nano-distillery and bar in Tooting Market.

Things move fast in Tooting, though, and it wasn't long before distilling had to move to premises in the Merton Abbey Mills complex and the market unit was transformed into Graveney Gin inside Tooting Market. In this tiny space you can sample craft gins from around the world, as well as sip Graveney cocktails.

As befits the small scale of the operation, Graveney uses a mere seven botanicals, all organic and ethically sourced, with the juniper influence quite apparent. But baobab and goji berries lend an African note, reflecting Victoria's South African roots, and every bottle contributes its mite to endangered African wildlife. Graveney has pledged 10% of all profits to Gearing up for Gorillas, a non-profit charity that protects, and educates the public about, the rare mountain gorillas of Virunga National Park (not a terribly good idea to go there, though; 160 rangers have been killed in the line of duty in the past twenty years).

Growth has meant that the original see-through label has been replaced by a cheerful paper wrap-round featuring a jungle scene and carrying a little bronze medallion embossed with the nano-batch and organic messages. Through all this comes a great sense of fun. As Victoria says on the website: 'My mantra is summed up in one word – fun! I have fun while making, talking and sharing Graveney Gin.'

Quite right, too. If you can't be a banker any longer, and eat roast swan and live in a mansion, why not make gin? It's worked for some notable successes in the craft distilling scene and there's every sign that Graveney will follow them to glory. That would be cool.

44

G'VINE FLORAISON

BRAND OWNER: EWG Spirits & Wine, Cognac, France

DISTILLERY: S.A.S. EuroWineGate, Villevert, Merpins, France

WEBSITE: www.escapetothegrape.com or www.g-vine.com

VISITOR CENTRE: No

STRENGTH: 40%

OTHER VARIANTS: Nouaison

G'Vine would like you to know five things about their gin. First, it's made in France from grape spirit. Second and uniquely, it uses the grape flower as a botanical. Third, there are two styles: the lighter Floraison (40%) and the more traditional Nouaison (43.9%). Fourth, they make it in the Charente region of Cognac. That feels more like a refinement of number one, but we'll let them off. And, finally, it's distilled by Jean-Sébastien Robicquet, who created it back in 2005. Well, someone has to make it, so I think they're padding the list here: let's call it three things.

But G'Vine is no longer the only gin distilled using a grape-based spirit (Madrid's 'urban distillery' Santamanía does this; so does Chilgrove in Chichester as well as the Menorcan Xoriguer). However, it was almost certainly the first new wave gin to do this, and it is genuinely unusual to find gin made in Cognac (though Citadelle are also there, using a more conventional wheat spirit).

Floraison is the more unusual and experimental of the two, more delicate and showing more of the influence of the grape flowers. Using them as a botanical really does seem to be unique, and presents unique challenges: for one thing, there is only a window of around a fortnight in which they can be picked before they become small grapes, which is what Nature had planned for them all along.

After studying oenology, and then training as a lawyer, Jean-Sébastien worked in the international cognac trade before returning to the family vineyards. So he brought the sensitivity of a trained winemaker to white spirits, observing that vodka and gin were growing far more rapidly than cognac and that their consumers were more open to innovation than the more traditionally orientated brandy drinker. It also didn't hurt that while cognac takes years to reach maturation, white spirits are ready much, much faster.

And so G'Vine was born. If you're not a very traditionally minded gin drinker you will probably prefer Floraison, whereas Nouaison will appeal more to the hard-core aficionado. The spicier, fuller flavour is influenced by a different balance of botanicals bringing the classic juniper and citrus notes to the fore.

Floraison, by contrast, may just be the gin to persuade vodka drinkers to try a grown-up drink. (Sorry, vodka drinkers, but you deserve it!)

HARRIS GIN

BRAND OWNER: Isle of Harris Distillers Ltd

DISTILLERY: Harris Distillery, Tarbert, Isle of Harris, Outer Hebrides

WEBSITE: www.harrisdistillery.com

VISITOR CENTRE: Yes

STRENGTH: 45%

OTHER VARIANTS: None

Apparently, I upset the people at the Harris Distillery who thought I had been 'disparaging' about their distillery in my most recent book *Whiskies Galore!*[1]. Well, I was a little cheeky about some of their marketing and sceptical about the wisdom of £5m of public sector support but I didn't think I was that critical – let's see if we can make up.

Although Harris itself is not easy to get to it's enjoying something of a tourist boom. However, the local economy is fragile, and permanent, long-term employment hard to find. The distillery was created, in part at least, to provide well-paid, skilled jobs (hence the investment of taxpayers' money) in a sustainable business that could work year-round to produce an internationally appealing product while also benefiting from the influx of affluent tourists. Happily, it seems to be working.

Eventually they'll launch a single malt whisky, but that takes a long time to mature and consumes much cash. So a small gin still was installed and Harris Gin was born. It was an immediate success; partly because of Harris's skilled and experienced marketing and brand management team but mainly because it's very good.

But before we get to that, a word or two on the bottle. It is, I have to say, extremely good-looking and satisfying to hold. There are many pleasing details in the get-up, including a Latin motto subtly embossed on the base, a simple and elegant label and a chunky wood and cork stopper. If you're paying nearly forty quid for your gin it's reasonable to expect a handsome presentation, and this doesn't disappoint. You won't want to put this in the recycling and I'd expect a good proportion of the bottles to live on as candle holders or water jugs.

The gin itself is quite sweet, beginning with plenty of juniper but evolving through citrus notes before herbal and floral flavours emerge and then the *pièce de résistance* – a sweet, complex and beguiling maritime note. This is Harris's *coup de théâtre*, its party trick, its unique selling proposition – local sugar kelp seaweed, collected by hand by a local diver – and it contributes to making a sensational Martini, because if you like the sugar kelp you can add more using the little bottle and dropper they'll sell you.

Honestly, it's one of my new favourites. Do you think they'll speak to me now?

---

[1] It's actually frightfully good; you should buy a copy

46

HAYMAN'S LONDON DRY

BRAND OWNER: Hayman Ltd

DISTILLERY: Hayman's, 8a Weir Road, Balham, London

WEBSITE: www.haymansgin.com

VISITOR CENTRE: Yes

STRENGTH: 41.2%

OTHER VARIANTS: Old Tom, Gently Rested, Sloe, Royal Dock

One could easily devote an entire book to Hayman's. Stand aside, newcomers; here we have the fifth generation of a family of distillers – gin aristocracy if you will. As you can see from the listing they make a wide variety of different expressions. Sadly, I've only room for one but all are well worth trying – these are 'true English gins', a subject on which Hayman's have strong opinions. Check out their 'Call Time on Fake Gins' online if you doubt that: they have raised the standard for juniper in an attempt to define the boundary between true gins and the other spirit drinks that masquerade under its name. It's noble work and all power to their elbow.

Their story starts in 1863 when the current chairman Christopher Hayman's great-grandfather James Burrough purchased a London gin rectifying business – their most famous brand then and now was Beefeater. Christopher joined in 1969 and was responsible for the distillation and production of Beefeater until 1987 when it was sold to Whitbread, then brewers (how things change – they stopped brewing in 2001 and today own Premier Inn and Costa Coffee).

But Whitbread and distilling didn't really get on, and a mere two years later they had sold all their whisky and gin operations. Hayman's successfully bought back the Fine Alcohols Division and Burrough's ended up owned by Pernod Ricard.

Thames Distillers subsequently produced the Hayman's brands, but you can't keep a true gin family down and soon they were distilling once again in Witham in Essex. Amongst other things, the Tiptree gin liqueurs are made there. Then, in March 2018 they opened their splendid new distillery in Balham, just four miles from where they started 150 years ago, operating three stills and working with just ten traditional botanicals.

Their Old Tom, having been discontinued at some time in the 1950s, was relaunched in November 2007 and is considered a reference point which defines the category, with a subtle sweetness derived as much from liquorice as the added sugar. For certain cocktails nothing else will do.

But the standard bearer is their classic London Dry which, since the move to Balham, has been subtly repackaged (very tasteful) and beefed up in strength. There are many London Dry gins but this is *primus inter pares*; the very quintessence of the style from a justly respected family company and Britain's senior gin dynasty.

HELSINKI GIN

BRAND OWNER: The Helsinki Distilling Company

DISTILLERY: Työpajankatu 2a R3, 00580
Helsinki, Finland

WEBSITE: www.hdco.fi

VISITOR CENTRE: Yes

STRENGTH: 47%

OTHER VARIANTS: None

Two Finns and an Irishman walked into a bar . . . No, actually that's not quite right. These two Finns and the Irishman built their own very funky bar in Teurastamo, which is an up-and-coming district of Helsinki – think Shoreditch and you'll get the general idea. Their building was a power plant for thirty years and afterwards a soap factory, a meatball factory, a car wash, a wine cellar and an architect's office.

But, very sensibly, there's now a bar on top of Helsinki Distilling Company's very own distillery where this energetic and talented team make some of the very nicest rye whiskey that it's been my pleasure to taste in a long time, aquavit, applejack, gin and distinctively Finnish gin liqueurs, and a thing called Helsinki Tyrnipontikka. I don't know what this is but having tasted it I'm happy to report it's just fine. Still can't pronounce it, though.

There's been an explosion of new craft distilleries in Finland (see also Napue from Kyrö and PyyGin from Teerenpeli) but they have learned their trade very quickly and are producing impressive products. This Helsinki Gin was the team's first release and it's gaining them new fans in a number of markets, including the UK.

It took a lot of determination to get the necessary permits and, in fact, this is Helsinki's first distillery in more than a century as the Finns explored their curious relationship with alcohol. Finnish has lots of drinking words – my favourite is *kalsarikännit*, which means to get drunk at home in your underpants, with no intention of doing anything else. They could almost be honorary Scots.

Nine hand-picked botanicals are blended with the purest Finnish water in the making of Helsinki Dry Gin. The unique taste, suggestive of the aromas of the Nordic forest with floral and citrus overtones, comes from Finnish lingonberries, rich Balkan juniper and Seville orange and lemon peels. Also found there are fennel and coriander seeds, orris root, angelica root and a small but important pinch of rose petals, resulting in a full-bodied and balanced gin. It is bottled without chill filtration so be aware that it may go a little hazy when served and, as the strength is a beefy 47%, note that you may go a little hazy as well once you have been served. Two large ones should just about do it. After that it's underpants time.

Their aimable master distiller Mikko Mykkänen puts his name on every bottle of Helsinki Gin. So would I, if I made it.

HENDRICK'S

BRAND OWNER: William Grant & Sons
DISTILLERY: Girvan, Ayrshire
WEBSITE: www.hendricksgin.com
VISITOR CENTRE: Under development
STRENGTH: 41.4%
OTHER VARIANTS: None

Hard though it is to believe, Hendrick's has only been with us since 1999, and wasn't launched in the UK until 2003, but the apothecary-style bottle and ingenious faux-Victorian marketing are powerfully suggestive of something a great deal older: the get-up has fooled at least one gin 'writer' into describing it as 'classic'. It's anything but.

As the website and promotional material are at great pains to insist this is a quite unusual product. But this is entirely in character for William Grant & Sons (think Glenfiddich and The Balvenie amongst others) who remain family-owned and determinedly independent. Since 1887 the company has followed its own path. Hendrick's is no exception: perhaps only Grant's would have named this brand after a senior family member's gardener, though it is said he tended the roses that inspired its distinctive taste.

The distilling process (sadly closed to the public though a visitor centre is under development) is quite unusual: Hendrick's uses a blend of spirits produced from a 1948 Carterhead still, and a vintage pot still dating to 1860. Both were bought at auction in 1966 by the late Charles Grant Gordon, who built the original Girvan distillery to produce grain whisky. He appears to have purchased them on something of a whim, but they were later restored to working order. The two stills produce strikingly different styles of gin due to their different construction and methods of distillation, whereupon the two spirits are blended together and then essences of Bulgarian rose petals and cucumber are added (they are too delicate a flavour to be distilled with the other botanicals).

The brand was something of a sensation and, together with Bombay Sapphire, may be credited with transforming the market. It has certainly been responsible for unleashing a range of less orthodox flavours on an unsuspecting world. This may well be deplored by purists (and, truth to tell, it's not my favourite) but there is no denying its immensely powerful influence in inspiring a new generation of boutique distillers.

I confess I'm quite conflicted about Hendrick's. I applaud its huge contribution to the category; I have the greatest of respect for its astute and remarkably consistent marketing; I recognise that it's a very well-made product from a highly respected company; but it's one which moves too far from traditional juniper-led gin for my palate.

I think of it as a gin for people who don't particularly like gin.

49

HERNÖ

BRAND OWNER: Hernö Brenneri AB

DISTILLERY: Hernö, Dala, Ångermanland, Sweden

WEBSITE: www.hernogin.com

VISITOR CENTRE: Yes

STRENGTH: 40.5%

OTHER VARIANTS: Navy Strength, Juniper Cask, Old Tom, Limited Editions

Apparently this is a 'Swedish gin miracle'. Big claim, but in a few short years Hernö have been busy collecting an impressive number of awards. The company was founded by Jon Hillgren, who was working in London as a bartender when he discovered gin (it wasn't lost – it's just that he didn't know much about it until then). Much experimentation and many trials later, Jon founded Hernö Gin Distillery in 2011, which proudly claims to be Sweden's first dedicated gin distillery and the world's northernmost (as we go to print, but on current trends it won't be long before someone starts distilling at the North Pole).

The distillery, built to resemble a traditional Swedish red-and-white painted wooden manor house, is home to Kierstin, a 250-litre Carl copper still, first installed on 29 May 2012 – I quote the entire date just to show the comparative youth of this operation.

I'm not entirely surprised that it does well in competitions, where more forceful and strongly flavoured products can stand out in an extended tasting. The 'Swedish Excellence' standard product is certainly an assertive, hot and spicy liquid which initially drinks stronger than its 40.5% abv. I can see how it might cut through jaded palates but, when I first wrote about this, I worried that the majority of its really big medals had come from a trade magazine competition and not the major international awards.

Well, that was then. Since the first edition of this book Hernö has gone on to collect significant plaudits from both the IWSC and the ISC. In fact, all the Hernö variants have been recognised, leading the brand's website to claim that Hernö Gin was 'the most awarded gin in Europe 2013–2017'.

So, if you like bold flavours you may well care for this. I think Jon Hillgren deserves a great deal of credit for creating a product that stands out from the mainstream and can generate an enthusiastic following of supporters. His other products, especially the Juniper Cask style, are highly innovative and well worth exploring. Rumour is that Hernö may release a sampling pack of four 20cl bottles of their different styles – that would make for a memorable vertical tasting and certainly goes straight onto my birthday list.

And in a couple of pages, after a short detour to the hills and harbours of bonny Galloway, we'll move on to another Swedish gin . . .

HILLS & HARBOUR

BRAND OWNER: Crafty Scottish Distillers Ltd

DISTILLERY: Crafty Distillery, Wigtown Road, Newton Stewart, Dumfries and Galloway

WEBSITE: www.craftydistillery.com

VISITOR CENTRE: Yes

STRENGTH: 40%

OTHER VARIANTS: None

$\mathcal{O}ne$ of the unforeseen consequences of the boom in craft distilleries has been an implied questioning of the myth of the 'Master Distiller'. The marketing gurus of the drinks industry had been keen to promote this idea, turning their production colleagues into minor rock stars possessed of esoteric knowledge and ancient, arcane skills known only to a privileged elite. The Master Distiller, it sometimes seemed, was a member of a shadowy and secretive cabal and it must be admitted that the drinks writing community were generally happy to go along with this whimsical notion.

But if anyone can set themselves up as a distiller and, with a little training and the right equipment, produce spirits that, in blind tasting, stand comparison with the established authorities then where stands the Master Distiller of old? All sorts of people are turning their hand to distilling these days – former surveyors, ex-bankers, farmers, even graphic designers – and making excellent, tasty products. Sometimes the product is gin or whisky and sometimes it's tourism, for direct sales to interested visitors – especially in an area popular with holidaymakers – are an essential part of the business model. So 'experiences' must be offered as well as elixirs, and here we have both.

The Crafty Distillery is run by Graham Taylor who, for fifteen years, was a designer (a very good one, as I have cause to know) but has swapped that profession for the long hours of craft distilling in his native Galloway. He seems happy, and so he should be because inside the rather tastefully distinctive bottle (he was a designer after all), we encounter a rather distinctively tasteful gin (see what I did there?).

Hills & Harbour reflects the secluded forests and coastlines of Galloway and, to prove it, Graham sent me a bit of a tree. It was from the noble fir, needles of which join bladderwrack seaweed and nine other botanicals in their stills. They're also keen to point out that they make their own wheat-based spirit from local grain, something which marks them out as serious distillers.

Perhaps, one day, even Master Distillers.

NB: At this point, I would like to stress that writing about spirits is altogether another matter. This requires immense dedication, years of unremunerative and thankless toil, and is not a profession to be entered into lightly. Or indeed, at all. There are quite enough drinks writers already, but I thank you for your interest.

51

HVEN

BRAND OWNER: Backafallsbyn AB

DISTILLERY: Backafallsbyn, Hven, Sweden

WEBSITE: www.hven.com

VISITOR CENTRE: Yes

STRENGTH: 40%

OTHER VARIANTS: Navy Strength

Pay attention, for this is going to get complex. Established in 2008 to create Swedish whisky, the Backafallsbyn distillery is Sweden's third-ever pot still distillery, part of a wider movement there to create artisanal spirits in what was traditionally a heavily regulated market, with stringent government controls. It's located on the tiny island of Hven, situated in Öresund, between Denmark and Sweden, which you can only reach by boat. With fewer than 350 inhabitants, think more of Jura than Islay.

So far, so simple. But wait. Oak aged gins are seen frequently enough these days, but Hven take the highly unusual step (it may even be unique) of aging their spirit in oak *before* it is redistilled into gin. First, they make their own organic wheat-based spirit and then vat it for twenty-four hours with their botanicals.

After that, the spirit is filtered off and filled into American oak casks, where it matures for eighteen months. Then, into the tall Hven stills it goes – lots of extended copper contact and reflux going on there, I would guess, as the stills have unusually tall necks. All that sounds unusual enough, but the distillery then rest the chosen final cut for another three months in steel vats. And then, at which point even the most obsessive of us would have cried 'enough', they distil it again before reducing it to a bottling strength of 40% abv, but without carbon or chill filtration.

So this isn't a 'barrel-aged' gin, but it is extraordinarily smooth, full flavoured and rich. Personally, I'd love to try it at 46% or even as a Navy Strength but I hesitate to tell someone this fanatical how to manage their business. The botanicals, including locally sourced juniper, comprise grains of paradise, citrus, aniseed, Guinea pepper, Sichuan pepper, calamus root, cardamom, cassia and Mauritian Bourbon vanilla (I did get a strong vanilla hit from this but assumed it was due to the pre-aging in American wood).

The flavours really do pop out very distinctly and clearly, but despite this Hven manages to be beautifully balanced and integrated. What's more, despite that time-consuming production method and rather charming packaging it's not absurdly expensive. UK websites offer this at around £32 for the 50cl bottle (equivalent to approximately £45 for a standard bottle). That's not cheap, but you'll want to sip and savour this most distinctive gin, which offers excellent value for the quality and presentation.

52

JAWBOX

BRAND OWNER: Jawbox Spirits Co. Ltd
DISTILLERY: The Echlinville Distillery,
62 Gransha Rd, Newtownards,
N. Ireland
WEBSITE: www.jawboxgin.com
VISITOR CENTRE: Yes
STRENGTH: 43%
OTHER VARIANTS: None

I detect the hand of marketing here. From the elaborate faux-Victorian labelling to the artfully crafted story, all the touch points (some marketing lingo for you there) have been carefully mediated to reflect brand messages – it's all 'graft and craft', if I might borrow one of their favourite lines.

Not that marketing is a bad thing. It paid my mortgage for long enough and this Jawbox does have a certain charm, not that it's going to let you forget it. The name, we are told, comes from the colloquial term for a Belfast sink and there's some rather romanticised 'good old days' copy on the label about the *craic* to be had around that piece of hard-working porcelain.

The gin is also described as 'Belfast Cut' which I'll admit is a new one on me. Since there hasn't, until very recently, been any distilling in Belfast since before the Second World War (and that of whiskey) perhaps the copywriter got a trifle carried away there. And it's actually distilled at the new Echlinville distillery, which is in Newtownards, some twenty miles or so from the city centre, on the rather splendid Echlinville Estate.

The whole thing is the brainchild of founder Gerry White who has brought his thirty and more years of drinks industry expertise to the Jawbox party, though several other parties have evidently joined in. But once past the surface blarney, there is a classic London Dry gin to be found: eleven botanicals, including local Black Mountain heather, all play their part in a big and bold, spicy and juniper-forward 43% spirit that makes a great G&T or cocktail base. The suggested serve is with ginger ale which was apparently first invented in Belfast – who knew?

There has been some significant investment in distilling plant and warehousing at Echlinville which, when it opened in 2013, was Northern Ireland's first licensed distillery in over 125 years. The shiny new stills are housed in an impressive glazed stillhouse and just one glance at the operation makes it clear that a free hand with the chequebook was required. Amongst other things, the old Dunville's whiskey brand has been revived here and, if you were of a flippant turn of mind, you could say that they've evidently thrown the kitchen sink at the distillery ... sorry.

Thing is, it's hard to ignore the value on offer. You should find Jawbox relatively easily at under £30 and for some decent small-batch production that's not to be sniffed at.

JUNIPERO

BRAND OWNER: Hotaling & Co.

DISTILLERY: Old Potrero Distillery,
San Francisco, California, USA

WEBSITE: www.hotalingandco.com

VISITOR CENTRE: Yes

STRENGTH: 49.3%

OTHER VARIANTS: Old Tom, Genevieve

The Old Potrero Distillery represents a very interesting phenomenon – a business in transition from a somewhat quirky craft brewing and distilling operation, very much the creation of one driven individual, to a larger, more corporate organisation. Junipero, one of the pioneers of small-batch gins, helped it get there.

It emerged from Anchor Brewing – a San Francisco craft brewer when the term was almost unknown – that had been saved from closure by Fritz Maytag, scion of a well-known domestic appliance company. Presumably brewing looked more fun than washing machines. Having got the brewery back on its feet, for some time prior to 1993 he had been toying with the idea of making rye whiskey, which had been almost forgotten as a style. Making it in a pot still, then a revolutionary concept, worked well and led the team to further experimentation and exploration of distilling's history. From that apparently endless process it was but a small step to gin, from which thinking emerged Junipero, arguably the USA's first craft gin, launched in April of 1996.

You probably don't need me to tell you that it's a very juniper-led gin (the name's a bit of a giveaway). At the time, the idea of launching a pot still-distilled craft gin was radical enough without wild experimentation in unusual botanicals. The gin revolution as we now know it was yet to start; this lit the fuse but stayed within well-recognised boundaries. The idea was not to break the rules but to create a well-crafted product on an unusual production basis. In that, Anchor succeeded, perhaps more fully than they could ever have anticipated.

At 49.3%, Junipero is a forceful character, well suited, like so many American craft gins, to mixing in a cocktail. There are twelve botanicals all worked together in the original small copper pot still. The exact mix is not disclosed but one can detect a pronounced citrus impact, as well as the influence of coriander and what I take to be liquorice. But mainly this is about the juniper.

Maytag retired from the business in 2010, and after various changes of ownership the company has more than tripled in size. Today, after Japan's Sapporo acquired the brewing arm and the Anchor trademark, the distillery company is known as Hotaling & Co. after turn-of-the-twentieth-century spirits dealer A. P. Hotaling. As if anyone knew.

54

KI NO BI KYOTO DRY

BRAND OWNER: Number One Drinks Company Ltd
DISTILLERY: Kyoto Distillery, Minami-ku, Kyoto, Japan
WEBSITE: www.kyotodistillery.jp
VISITOR CENTRE: No (VR tour on website)
STRENGTH: 45.7%
OTHER VARIANTS: Sei, Tea, Navy Strength

This is – remarkably – Japan's first artisan gin distillery and it's said to be the first distillery of any sort that has ever operated in historic Kyoto. That's remarkable enough, but what is really exceptional is that the Kyoto distillery is owned and operated by a British team. It's the brainchild of Marcin Miller and David Croll who have form with their successful Number One Drinks Company as an importer of rare Japanese whiskies into Europe.

Everything about it reflects their love and respect for Japanese life and culture: their young distiller Alex Davies may have lived and worked in England until immersing himself in Japan but Ki No Bi's distinctive glass bottles are hand-blown by craftspeople in Osaka's Sakai district and the screenprinted label – an elegant floral design displaying the gin's name, which means 'beauty of the seasons', in Japanese characters and Roman letters – is a collaboration with Kira Karacho, Kyoto's oldest maker of *karakami* (paper printed with woodblock patterns), who is based in an atelier founded in 1624.

With no tradition of gin distilling in Japan, stills were imported from Germany but the key ingredients are distinctively Japanese. Unusually, the neutral base spirit is made from rice and the eleven botanicals are sourced from in and around Kyoto. Juniper leads, of course, for this is a proper dry gin but orris, ginger, bamboo leaves, red perilla, lemon and yuzu peel, sansho pepper, kinome leaves, Gyokuro green tea and hinoki wood emphasise the Japanese heritage.

While gin may not have been distilled previously in Japan, it was not unknown and Ki No Bi was rapidly taken up by the famously demanding Tokyo mixologists. Further limited editions have followed. Such was its success that initial supplies to the UK were limited but you should now find bottles in better specialists. At around £45, it's not cheap, of course, but this is an exceptional product from a deeply committed team.

And it seems to have started a trend. This may have been Japan's first gin but the country's two much larger competitors soon launched their own expressions (and very good they are, too). Coincidence? Well, good timing certainly and testimony to the thought and planning that characterises every aspect of this impressive operation.

55

KINTYRE

BRAND OWNER: Beinn an Tuirc Distillers Ltd

DISTILLERY: Beinn an Tuirc, Torrisdale Castle Estate, Kintyre

WEBSITE: www.kintyregin.com

VISITOR CENTRE: Yes – from autumn 2018

STRENGTH: 43%

OTHER VARIANTS: None

Torrisdale Castle is on the Kintyre peninsula, between the splendidly named Grogport and Campbeltown, once a major centre for the distilling of Scotch whisky. It's a rather lovely part of Scotland, not least because it isn't heavily visited by tourists – though I daresay the castle would like a few more for their self-catering cottages (the servants' quarters look nice).

The 1,200-acre estate remains in family hands. Once there would have been servants, lots of them, but today properties like this have to be self-sustaining and the Macalister Hall family have been ingenious and creative in making the estate relevant to the twenty-first century, even if the lady of the house has to clean the holiday lets herself.

Torrisdale now features a bio-mass heating system, fuelled by wood from the grounds; a hydroelectric scheme (it rains a lot on Kintyre); and, most recently, a gin distillery. Beinn an Tuirc – it means the Hill of the Wild Boar – proudly describe themselves as 'sustainable distillers', based on the fact that they generate their own electricity; use local spring water and two of their own botanicals; and, for every case of gin sold, plant a tree on the estate (which, in years to come, will doubtless be chopped down to feed the bio-mass boiler). A percentage of profits will support community projects and local business start-ups through a planned charitable foundation, which is only fair. After all, our taxes helped to build the distillery through the grant-making largesse of the Highlands and Islands Enterprise agency who assisted the project.

So, that's a tick in all the right boxes, then, but is the gin actually any good? Well, they have all the proper kit (a smart, purpose-built German rig named Big Don after a late family member) and a recipe developed with help from the team behind Harris Gin. Add these credentials to the unique estate-grown botanicals, namely Icelandic moss and sheep sorrel; throw in some smart packaging (another family member owns a design agency) and a great story; and it almost doesn't matter.

But fortunately, I can report that it's a well-made and full-flavoured offering with an excellently balanced nose and creamy mouthfeel. It has a long and agreeably spicy finish and, to its credit, avoids some of the more outlandish flavour notes that characterise some of the new small-batch producers. It performs well in a classic G&T. It's not swamped by the mixer, and at 43% is a great cocktail base.

KIRKJUVAGR

BRAND OWNER: Orkney Distilling Ltd

DISTILLERY: The Orkney Distillery, Ayre Road, Kirkwall, Orkney

WEBSITE: www.orkneydistilling.com

VISITOR CENTRE: Yes

STRENGTH: 43%

OTHER VARIANTS: Arkh-Angell Storm Strength

Well, if you needed one, there are now at least *three* gin reasons to go to Orkney (as well as Highland Park and Scapa distilleries for the whisky enthusiast in your life) as gin seems to have taken over these lovely islands. There is the Orkney Gin Company and the tiny Deerness Distillery, but I'm awarding the crown to the Kirkjuvagr gin from Orkney Distilling, who are based in Kirkwall. Incidentally, Orkney is somewhere you should visit at least once in your life but, be warned, once you've been you will want to go straight back.

Now, the Kirkjuvagr team would be the first to admit that their gin actually began life at Strathearn in Perthshire where they worked to develop the recipe and distil the initial batches, but very soon they opened a splendid purpose-built distillery and visitor centre in a smart new building right by Kirkwall harbour (it's no coincidence that the distillery's energetic founder Stephen Kemp and his wife Aly own a substantial construction company).

It's also no coincidence that the site is very close to the point where visitors from the many cruise ships that call into Orkney disembark. They can carry as many as 5,700 passengers, all of them desperate for an insight into island life. And, if that can be accompanied by a tasty G&T, well, perhaps Skara Brae can wait.

But for all that, the product is deeply rooted in Orkney. The Kemps worked closely with the island's highly regarded Agronomy Institute and make extensive use of local botanicals, even to the extent of incorporating some Orkney-grown bere (an early landrace strain of barley) in their gin. To match the early batches distilled at Strathearn, the same type and size of Hoga still from Portugal has been installed but, planning for success, there are two rather than one. A larger still might have been cheaper and more efficient, but trials suggested that the final product didn't match up so two 100-litre stills seemed the way forward. It's typical of their demanding and rigorous approach.

It was also very much an Orkney effort, which has enjoyed a good deal of local support, with graphics by a local designer and Louis Wright, Head of Production, hailing from Kirkwall itself. As it ramps up to full production Kirkjuvagr will be a welcome addition to our shelves here, always assuming that those thirsty cruise-ship passengers leave any for the rest of us to enjoy.

57

LAKES

BRAND OWNER: The Lakes Distillery Company Ltd
DISTILLERY: The Lakes Distillery, Cumbria
WEBSITE: www.lakesdistillery.com
VISITOR CENTRE: Yes
STRENGTH: 43.7%
OTHER VARIANTS: Explorer

Another day, another gin; another Oslo bottle. That's the trade name for this squat bottle which makes a regular appearance on the craft distilling scene (some bigger producers, such as Bruichladdich, even use it for whisky though their gin gets its own custom bottle). I've lost count of the number of these that I've seen.

Now, don't get me wrong: it's a very handsome bottle, simple and elegant, easy to use, and I realise that the costs of a custom bottle are prohibitive for small operators. But (not to pick on Lakes because they're far from alone) the problem surely is one of distinct identity and stand-out shelf appeal. If lots of people use the same bottle then the label has to work extra hard. You might even come to pity the poor designer, which is not a sentence I ever expected to write. Anyway, as it's what's in the bottle that really counts and having made that point, I'll move on.

Lakes is a new distillery, having opened as recently as November 2014. It's based in and around some charming nineteenth-century farm buildings and seems to fit very naturally and comfortably into its landscape. MD and founder Paul Currie has family connections with the Arran distillery in Scotland (they make whisky there, of course) and has recruited some serious whisky distilling talent to run the operation here. It appears that they know a thing or two about making gin as well. Lakes is a slightly sweet drop that uses local botanicals such as bilberry, heather and meadowsweet to create a gin that is both smooth and engagingly complex. Juniper is ever present, naturally, but in this case it's locally sourced from the surrounding fells, and water comes from the River Derwent, so this is as artisanal and local as you get.

With the considerable Lake District tourist trade to boost their visitor numbers, all of them no doubt anxious to take home a souvenir rather more appealing than a copy of De Quincey's *Recollections*, the distillery's fame should spread far and wide.

Lakes show convincingly how far the new wave of distillers have advanced. This is a sophisticated, balanced and utterly convincing product that can hold its head up in any company. I'd suggest serving it just 50:50 with your tonic of choice. At 43.7% it's got plenty of mouthfeel, weight and body, and it's a shame to drown that with too much effervescence.

58

LANGLEY'S NO. 8

BRAND OWNER: Charter Brands Ltd

DISTILLERY: The Langley Distillery, Langley Green, Warley, West Midlands

WEBSITE: www.langleysgin.com

VISITOR CENTRE: No

STRENGTH: 41.7%

OTHER VARIANTS: Old Tom, First Chapter

Langley's Distillery was founded almost a century ago by the Palmer family and, since 1920, they have been developing and producing some of the finest award-winning gins in the world, now including their own (it's number 71 if you can't wait). In fact, quite a number of the gins listed here start life in the West Midlands, in much the same way as those I've included from Thames Distillers. It's a substantial operation, with six stills, and, though arguably less famous than Thames, is equally well regarded by those in the know.

But, as this carries the distillery's own name, you'd be forgiven for thinking it was their own brand. Not so: it's another contract-distilled gin, this time for the Charter Brands company who wanted a gin for gentlemen; their theory being that many recently launched gins were too girly. That's not *quite* how they put it but you get the idea – and you can make your own mind up.

The 'No. 8' tag came about because eight botanicals are used and the eighth was the winning sample in their development trials, prior to the 2013 launch. It's made in Connie, a 4,000-litre English copper pot still from 1960 by John Dore & Co. that wouldn't seem out of place in a single malt whisky distillery. Incidentally, founded back in the 1830s, they are said to be the oldest pot still producers in the world. Unusually, the botanicals aren't steeped in the neutral grain spirit prior to distillation but placed directly in the still immediately prior to firing (men, eh, they just can't wait; gotta rush into everything).

The high-strength gin then leaves Warley for Witham in Essex where it is bottled at 41.7%. In researching all this I happened to note the curious coincidence that both Warley and Witham are mentioned in the Domesday Book. I don't suppose that's of the slightest significance, but it just struck me as curious and interesting. There's no charge – don't mention it.

What we can't avoid mentioning, though, is the 'gin for men' theory. Mark Dawkins, one of the men behind Charter Brands, has been so bold as to suggest that men have 'less of a sweet palate' and instead look for 'big flavours, complexity, and a sophisticated flavour profile'. So, my wife being a total poppet, I thought I'd ask her.

'Interesting,' she said, 'but I don't want any more.' So there we have it: conclusive proof that my wife is definitely a woman.

59

LUSSA

BRAND OWNER: Lussa Drinks Company LLP
DISTILLERY: Lussa, The Stables, Ardlussa, Isle of Jura
WEBSITE: www.lussagin.com
VISITOR CENTRE: Visits by appointment only
STRENGTH: 42%
OTHER VARIANTS: None

Once upon a time I nearly visited the Lussa distillery. Don't mock, because this is a most un-get-at-able place. That's what George Orwell said when he escaped here after the Second World War to write *1984*, and he was right. It's less time, trouble and expense to fly to New York.

But then, like me, you wouldn't get to see this distillery in a stable and meet the three lady adventurers behind Lussa. I did get within twenty miles, though I was actually on Jura to write about the whisky that's made there and learnt of the gin, which had only then been launched, quite by accident. Unfortunately, there was no time to make the return trip on the challenging single-track road and still get back for the ferry.

Jura is a funny old place, famously home to one road; 200 people; 6,000 red deer; and an Australian multi-millionaire who is building a private golf course at a reputed cost of £55m. Most of the land is given over to deer forests and the island is split into a few very large sporting estates held by rich absentee landlords. One estate, however, to the north end of the island is owned by the Fletcher family who are said to be the only owners in permanent residence.

Anyhow, Claire Fletcher who originally came here to shoot a video for the KLF (their relationship with Jura is altogether another story) and stayed, has joined forces with two friends Georgina Kitching and Alicia Macinnes. With a natty little Portuguese still to feed, they grow, gather and distil local botanicals that make up their adventure in gin. They have planted juniper bushes, harvest pine needles and sea lettuce, and grow other botanicals, fifteen in all, in polytunnels and greenhouses around the island to create a full-bodied and earthy gin with floral and citrus flavours. There are some lovely field notes on the website (let's face it, this is as close as you're going to get).

However, if you do manage a trip to Jura – and it's something I'd definitely recommend – you can arrange a distillery tour with a bottle to take home for a perfectly modest £45. I hope they succeed. Living on an island, especially one as extreme as Jura, is not my idea of fun. It takes a very special personality to hack it, so to combine that with growing a business is quite admirable.

So, Claire and friends – respect! (They like it if I say that . . .)

60

MAKAR

BRAND OWNER: The Glasgow Distillery
Company Ltd
DISTILLERY: Glasgow Distillery, Glasgow
WEBSITE: www.glasgowdistillery.com
VISITOR CENTRE: No
STRENGTH: 43%
OTHER VARIANTS: Old Tom, Oak Aged, Mulberry Aged

Although this is a brand new distillery, it's backed by some serious and well-connected drinks industry personalities and is evidently well funded. If you doubt that, just take a look at the stylish customised bottle. Designs and a new bespoke glass mould don't come cheap, so this is a big statement of intent from the newly arrived Glasgow gin, named Makar, the Scots term for a poet or bard.

The venture, not to be confused with another rival Glasgow distillery which is about to start production on the banks of the River Clyde, is located in Hillington Business Park to the west of the city. Funding has come from a group of Asian food and drink investors as well as a £130,000 Regional Selective Assistance grant. Apparently, a total investment of 'several million' pounds was involved.

Though whisky stills will be installed, the Makar gin is produced in its brand new 450-litre Christian Carl still, a pot still with a seven-plate column that has been christened Annie. The still alone is a £100,000 piece of equipment, capable of producing some 300 bottles from each seven-hour distillation run. There is a first-year target of some 10,000 bottles, which is ambitious – but why not?

Many fine gins are made in Scotland, and this looks set fair to join that number. A traditionally styled dry gin, it's loaded with juniper berries and uses seven other botanicals: angelica root, rosemary, liquorice, peppercorns, coriander seeds, cassia bark and lemon peel. The distinctive bottle will certainly stand out on back bars, an increasingly important point of difference as the market for small-batch gins becomes ever more congested. The seven sides of the bottle are intended to represent the seven botanicals added to the juniper – and also make the bottle easy to grip and pour, which will no doubt be welcomed by harried bar staff.

Head distiller Jack Mayo, a graduate of the Heriot-Watt University's distilling course, is in charge of production and will be joined by David Robertson, ex-Macallan and Whyte & Mackay, on a consultancy basis once whisky production begins.

The taste is clearly, and very properly, described as 'juniper-led'; very markedly a world away from the lighter, more floral style of some new gins. Makar is bold, assertive and forceful – no mean gin, in fact.

61

MALFY CON LIMONE

BRAND OWNER: Biggar & Leith LLC

DISTILLERY: Torino Distillati, via Montegrappa 37, Moncalieri, Turin, Italy

WEBSITE: www.malfygin.com

VISITOR CENTRE: No

STRENGTH: 41%

OTHER VARIANTS: Originale, Rosa, Con Arianca

Developed for Biggar & Leith, a US-based drinks agency with distant Scottish roots, Malfy is part of a small stable of brands that they own and distribute. Their mission, they say, is to work with 'established, family-owned distilleries who are dedicated to innovation and quality [and to] search the globe for brands whose bottles transmit the personality and stories of the people who make them'.

Nice work if you can get it, especially if it takes you to Italy and some tasty gins. The Malfy range is distilled by the Vergnano family in Moncalieri, Italy, using an unusual stainless-steel vacuum still and unique Italian ingredients. They've been distilling there since 1906 but make the curious claim that back in the eleventh century monks on the Salerno coast added *ginepro* (juniper) and other botanicals to base alcohol and that accordingly gin began in Italy. I'm not sure that would go down very well in Holland, but, frankly, who cares because this is very far removed from anything an eleventh-century monk would cook up.

I'm a sucker for citrus-led gins, hence the decision to lead with this expression, rather than the other three in the family. Tasted neat, it's quite a robust spirit but this isn't one for thoughtful sipping – rather this screams of *la dolce vita*, or even *dolce far niente*, the sweet art of doing nothing . . .

I could see myself doing nothing with a glass or two of this on board a Riva Rivamare, speeding past the Villa Oleandra in Laglio on Lake Como and raising a glass to the locals.[1] Or possibly in some chic bar in Portofino or Santa Margherita Ligure, people-watching and happily contemplating my dinner. It's a languorous, luxurious and indulgent drop that is very heavy on the lemons – perhaps some seafood is suggested?

As far as the gin itself is concerned, it's not overly complex, employing just six botanicals and a wheat-based alcohol which has been steeped in a blend of Sfusato Amalfi coastal lemons and Sicilian lemon peel. The still is unusual, however; the principle at work being that the freshness and vitality of the citrus is preserved by low-temperature distillation. The result won't necessarily appeal to the juniper loyalists (who won't like the packaging either) but it is different and adds something new and welcome to the gin-drinking repertoire, even if the creation story upsets our Dutch friends.

---

[1] It's George Clooney's house.

62

MARTIN MILLER'S

BRAND OWNER:	The Reformed Spirits Company
DISTILLERY:	The Langley Distillery, Langley Green, Warley, West Midlands
WEBSITE:	www.martinmillersgin.com
VISITOR CENTRE:	No
STRENGTH:	40%
OTHER VARIANTS:	Westbourne Strength, 9 Moons

This highly awarded gin was one of the pioneers of the new wave of premium gins, and has been notably successful since its launch in 1999. It's probably an inspiration to today's craft distillers hoping to emulate its apparently effortless rise to fame.

The eponymous Martin Miller was a true English eccentric – bon viveur, photographer, author, publisher of *Miller's Antique Guides*, hotel proprietor and probably half a dozen other things as well – who apparently came up with the idea for his gin in 1998, after finding that the gins then on the market fell short of his discriminating standards. So, he decided to create his own. As you do. Well, you do now, but back then things were different: this was quite a radical proposition.

Two things make this stand out: first, the distillation. It's not that Martin Miller's employs a huge number of botanicals, or some arcane ingredient that no one has ever heard of; no, they simply split the process into two separate distillations. The juniper and the 'earthier' botanicals along with the dried lime peel are distilled first, then the citrus peels, combining both distillates later. This balances the signature notes of juniper, and the bright, refreshing notes of citrus. Again, not so unusual today, but somewhat unorthodox fifteen years ago. It does mean, however, that Martin Miller's doesn't qualify as a London gin.

The next step remains, I think, unique. The high-strength distillate is reduced to drinking strength with water from Iceland. It seems like a lot of trouble to go to (in fact, you might almost consider it a gimmick) but the company argues that normal demineralised water is 'dead' despite accounting for around 50–60% of the contents.

According to the company, Icelandic Spring Water (they have their own spring now) is 'simply the purest and softest naturally occurring water to be found on the planet', which qualities make it perfect for blending gin. All this shipping water across the high seas might strike you as expensive and so you'd expect Martin Miller's to be pricey. Actually, you can find it widely available for £25 or less; not the cheapest then, but hardly overpriced. The curiously named 9 Moons is cask aged in Iceland.

Lots more information on their generally excellent website, and thankfully they've dropped the slightly morbid 'Ask Martin' page now that the fellow has gone to the great cocktail bar in the sky – where I imagine he's shaking things up and thoroughly enjoying himself.

63

MONKEY 47

BRAND OWNER: Pernod Ricard

DISTILLERY: Zum Wilden Affen,
Lossburg, Germany

WEBSITE: www.Monkey47.com

VISITOR CENTRE: By appointment only

STRENGTH: 47%

OTHER VARIANTS: Sloe, Distiller's Cut

Here's something clearly put together by someone quite obsessive. I mean that in a good way, because I really did love every 'touch point' (more marketing jargon there for you) about the brand even before I opened the bottle.

And then I positively squealed with pleasure because there is a little silver-coloured metal collar mounted on the cork, and, if you squint at it, you will find a Latin motto engraved there. *Ex pluribus unum*, it reads, which I take to mean 'out of many, one' – a reference no doubt to the forty-seven different botanicals (including *six* different peppers – I mean, come on) that go into this uniquely German gin which, as you will have guessed, is bottled at 47% abv. And, if you look even more closely, the metal collar is exquisitely engraved and there are delicate little crosses separating the text. You really have to be slightly mad to go to this trouble – and I love it.

You might think the bottle owes something to Hendrick's and the label to Elephant (or perhaps *vice versa*), but the product is unique. Of course, every product is unique, but this is really different. Their website is a thing of joy, on which you can happily spend hours reading about many different species of monkey, the jazz of Oscar Peterson, cork trees, Eddie the Eagle, many, many different cocktail recipes and their history, various different botanicals and the origins of Monkey 47. Incredibly, it can be traced to the personal recipe of a British RAF officer, Wing Commander Montgomery Collins, who settled in the Black Forest in the 1950s with the aim of becoming a watchmaker.

Fortunately for us, he apparently wasn't very good at it, so opened a guesthouse instead, which he named the Wild Monkey in honour of Max, a monkey he had sponsored in Berlin Zoo immediately after the war (so, technically, a captive monkey). There he attempted to recreate English gin, but with added local ingredients.

Thinking about all that, he must have been a true British eccentric. His spirit (pun intended) has been captured by founder Alexander Stein and his splendidly hirsute master distiller Christoph Keller, who, in recreating Collins' recipe, makes what wine critic Robert Parker called 'the greatest gin I have ever tasted'. Astonishingly, after distillation, the spirit rests for three months in earthenware crocks before it's reduced for bottling. I told you they were obsessive.

A highly distinctive product then, but a wonderful one.

64

NAPUE

BRAND OWNER: Kyrö Distillery Company

DISTILLERY: Kyrö Distillery, Oltermannintie 6,
61500 Isokyrö, Finland

WEBSITE: www.kyrodistillery.com

VISITOR CENTRE: Yes

STRENGTH: 46.3%

OTHER VARIANTS: Koskue

You wouldn't think being judged the best gin in the world for gin and tonic would be a problem, would you? Especially if around 150 other gins had entered and the award was coming from the International Wine & Spirit Competition who had created the IWSC Gin & Tonic Trophy in 2015 for the very first time.

But if you've just opened your distillery, you really intended to make great rye whiskey and you are quite picky about using some seasonal local botanicals for the gin a ten-fold increase in demand is definitely one of those #firstworldproblems. There's a further twist of course: you can't be sure that the new sales are essentially driven by curiosity and will be a one-off, after which demand will fall back to normal.

Finnish gin might, after all, just prove to be a flash in the pan – a novelty, after which the fickle customers move on to the next new thing or the latest award winner. That's the problem with awards, after all, they do set rather a high bar. Fortunately, though, everything turned out well for 'the rye rye gentlemen', as they style themselves. You can see rather more of them than you might wish, running naked through a field of the stuff, on their website and promotional literature.

But credit where credit's due. Kyrö really pioneered Finnish gin and deserve all the plaudits. As relatively early entrants into the small-scale distilling business they planned thoroughly and committed themselves fully to what they were doing – no tiny Portuguese stills off the web for them, they got straight into business with a quality 1,200-litre pot, which is one reason why the surge in demand could be handled smoothly enough.

As to the name, it commemorates the Battle of Napue (1714) where, unfortunately, around half of the resident male population died at the hands of their Russian foes in the Great Northern War (the Finns and the Russians haven't always been the best of chums; and I really don't want to think about the post-battle fate of the local females, Peter the Great having instructed his troops to lay waste to the whole area).

It's a curious date to pick to launch your distillery – think of a Scottish gin called Flodden and you get the picture – but according to the ever-reliable Wikipedia these terrible collective memories live on and the Finnish saying, 'A Russian is a Russian even if fried in butter' reflects this gruesome history. Very tasty gin, though.

65

NB

BRAND OWNER: NB Distillery Ltd.

DISTILLERY: North Berwick, East Lothian

WEBSITE: www.nbdistillery.com

VISITOR CENTRE: Yes

STRENGTH: 42%

OTHER VARIANTS: Navy Strength

N.B. *Nota bene.* It's the Latin for 'note well', a phrase which first appeared in text around 1721. 'Pay attention' it says.

And if we were in Scotland we might remember that Scotland once more or less happily referred to itself as NB, 'North Britain', hence the nomenclature of Edinburgh's grandest of grand railway hotels, the North British. Today it has sadly rebranded itself into the anodyne Balmoral Hotel. Which, as any Scot could tell you, ought by rights to be on Deeside.

NB also stands for North Berwick, a pleasant seaside town right on the Forth Estuary, about twenty-five miles east of Edinburgh and once a fashionable seaside resort. I have fond memories of North Berwick because in another life I played a role in establishing the town's principal attraction, the Scottish Seabird Centre.

And now it has something else – its very own distillery; a little one, with a John Dore still (not many of those about), making around one hundred litres per batch of NB Gin. It's a pretty straight-along-the-line London Dry gin, using just eight botanicals: juniper, coriander seed, angelica root, grains of paradise, lemon peel, cassia bark, cardamom and orris root. As you might expect, it's pretty much old school in style (nothing wrong with that), with plenty of juniper and orange notes, and bottled at a sensible 42% abv.

The distillery is the brainchild of husband and wife team Steve and Viv Muir, who have taken a very hands-on role at their micro-distillery, since launching it in October 2013. It's found a ready local acceptance and even made it into some export markets, despite the rather basic packaging. Oh, all right, it's minimalist, or retro or something. It does come in a box, if you're concerned about that kind of thing.

I'd rate this a very decent cocktail gin. Apparently Charles Maxwell of Thames Distillers advised on the development tasting panel, which was pretty decent of him, and rated it 'a very fine gin that was extremely likeable'. It's since won Silver in the Gin Masters competition.

So, you see, NB does stand for 'pay attention' after all. Given a decent sea breeze behind it I expect to see more of NB Gin.

66

NIKKA COFFEY

BRAND OWNER: Nikka Whisky Distilling Co. Ltd

DISTILLERY: Miyagikyo Distillery, 1 Nitsuka, Aoba-ku, Sendai-shi, Miyagi-ken, Japan

WEBSITE: www.nikka.com/eng/products/spirits/coffeygin

VISITOR CENTRE: Yes (Japanese language only)

STRENGTH: 47%

OTHER VARIANTS: None

Not 'coffee' but Coffey, a nineteenth-century Irish Excise officer turned distiller who, in 1830, patented an improved design for a continuous still. There were other similar stills operating around this date, but Coffey's proved the best and stood the test of time. In fact, though his very first examples were made of wood, an original example is still running in Guyana where it makes rum.

Today there are multi-column designs offering greater efficiency and producing a purer spirit. But the old two-column still, originally imported from Scotland more than fifty years ago, operated by Nikka at Miyagikyo produces a spirit with greater character and texture. Nikka is best known for its whiskies and for most of that time the still has been employed by them to make the grain whisky they need for their blends. However, in 2012 the venerable old apparatus came out of the shadows with the release of an unusual single grain whisky. This has been followed by their Coffey Gin and Vodka.

So the gin starts from a rich and silky spirit with maize and malt distilled separately and then precisely blended to create a base spirit. The botanicals include Japanese citrus such as yuzu, kabosu, hirami lemon and amanatsu, a touch of apples and the tangy Japanese sansho pepper, with juniper in there as you would expect. However, in what seems to be emerging as a distinct style in Japanese gins, the botanicals are divided into three groups: sansho pepper, fruit, and herbs and spices, and distilled separately. The herbs and spices are distilled in a regular pot still, but the citrus and pepper are distilled at low pressure to maintain more of their delicate flavours.

The resulting spirits are blended, but the dominant note comes from the various citrus components, which make this fresh, fruity and very refreshing, though with plenty of weight due to the 47% bottling strength (a contributor to the £40+ UK retail price).

It's probably worth remarking that not everyone will care for the strong citrus-forward nose and taste of this gin and the subsequent peppery notes, but if you want something a little out of the ordinary, something that will stand up to the inevitable dilution of a G&T or classic cocktail, then this could well be for you. One idea might be to get a bottle of this, Ki No Bi and Roku and serve them blind in a Japanese gin tasting evening.

67

OLD ENGLISH

BRAND OWNER:	Hammer & Son, Fredericksberg, Denmark
DISTILLERY:	The Langley Distillery, Langley Green, Warley, West Midlands
WEBSITE:	www.oldenglishgin.com
VISITOR CENTRE:	No
STRENGTH:	44%
OTHER VARIANTS:	None

Here's an odd thing: gin in a champagne bottle, made to a recipe dating from 1783 that is apparently kept in a safe. I do wonder why marketing people imagine these things are important or why they bother to tell us stuff like that. They must imagine we're captivated by these romantic stories and believe that they cast a soft, comforting glow of provenance and heritage onto their products. Oh wait, we are, and they do.

Old English is a stellar creation from the Great Dane Henrik Hammer, in which he is attempting to suggest how English (as opposed to Hollands, i.e. Dutch) gin might have looked and tasted in the eighteenth century. He noted that England was the largest importer of champagne back then (we still get through a fair amount) and hypothesised that bottles, being expensive objects at the time, would have been taken to gin shops to be refilled with a drop of kill-grief. It's a perfectly reasonable guess, I suppose, though what archaeologists and social historians would make of it I have no idea.

How accurately it replicates the gin of 1783 I wouldn't care to speculate. The recipe is doubtless authentic, but so many other things will have changed: the quality of the base spirit and botanicals and the detailed control of the process to mention but two. But then again, it doesn't really matter – what counts is whether or not today this counts as a decent gin.

It's a distilled gin, that's to say sugar is added after the distillation, which has used a fairly conventional mix of botanicals: juniper, coriander, lemon, orange, angelica, cassia, liquorice, cinnamon, orris root, nutmeg and cardamom, all distilled in a 100% English wheat pure grain spirit in Langley's Angela still.

Between Hammer and the team at Langley's they do know their stuff, and Old English has collected a number of impressive awards in high-class competition. Strictly speaking, this is an Old Tom but perhaps not as sweet as some. So, a decent replica of a 200-year-old-plus recipe, but personally I would have passed on the driven cork – faithfulness to the original can go too far and you're unlikely to drink the bottle at a sitting.

In today's age of responsible drinking that would be taking eighteenth-century authenticity a step too far. I couldn't possibly condone that, boys and girls, so please don't try it at home.

OPIHR

BRAND OWNER: Quintessential Brands
DISTILLERY: G & J Distillers, Warrington
WEBSITE: www.opihr.com
VISITOR CENTRE: No
STRENGTH: 40%
OTHER VARIANTS: None

Right, before we get started on this quirky new gin from Master Distiller Joanne Moore (clearly a lady with a restless and inventive mind and responsible for a number of interesting products), let's begin by saluting the marketing brain behind this.

For surely this is a marketing creation: the get-up is very pleasing; both bottle and label design are deceptively simple (that takes a lot of skill, believe me); and the whole package has a tactile quality that's hard to resist. They call it 'shelf appeal' in the trade. Someone has then come up with a load of half-believable guff on the website and back label describing Opihr as 'a legendary region famed for its wealth and riches which prospered during the reign of King Solomon. The King regularly received cargoes of gold, silver and spices from Opihr and whilst its exact location remains a mystery, it is thought to have been in the Orient along the ancient Spice Route'. Well, I suppose since the whole thing is a legend it could as well have been in Timbuktu or darkest Neasden for that matter (possibly not Neasden). It's generally spelt Ophir; I haven't the slightest idea why they saw fit to change it.

Opihr – it's pronounced 'o-peer' by the way, though under the influence of H. Rider Haggard I still badly want to spell it Ophir – is apparently targeted at 21–35-year-olds with a sense of adventure. That would seem to rule me out. It's certainly not going to appeal to the Jaguar-driving golf-club member who could be considered the archetypal gin drinker (though I don't fit in there either). Whatever, as I have been told adventurous 24–35-year-olds might say.

Right there on the label, centre front, are the words 'Oriental Spiced'. So, the mighty hit of cardamom and pepper that envelops your nose as you open the bottle shouldn't come as a surprise, even if the idea of a spiced gin is mildly shocking. With its recent releases, brand owners Quintessential really are pushing at our understanding of what gin should be.

I think I part company here. Not that this isn't interesting and different – and I'd urge you to try it, because it may just be your personal treasure galleon – but because for me the spice notes of cardamom, cumin and coriander are overwhelming and unsubtle. In fact, to be honest, I'm not sure I can really distinguish them individually.

Perhaps I should be more adventurous. I still think it's a very nice pack, though.

69

OXFORD DRY

BRAND OWNER:	Still on the Hill Ltd
DISTILLERY:	The Oxford Artisan Distillery (TOAD), South Park, Oxford
WEBSITE:	www.spiritoftoad.com
VISITOR CENTRE:	Yes
STRENGTH:	41.2%
OTHER VARIANTS:	Physic Gin, Ashmolean

I must confess to some slight concern when I learned that the neophyte distillers behind Oxford's first-ever distillery (can that really be true, I wondered) designed their own equipment. That twinge of apprehension only grew on hearing that they turned to a firm of railway engineers to help build their unorthodox stills, insisting that they incorporate an old ship's porthole into the design. Most folk go to some stillmakers and rummage through their catalogue.

My brow was ever more deeply furrowed by TOAD's insistence on heritage grain; the knowledge that the distillery's founder lives on an old barge; and that their master distiller was self-taught in his own illegal speakeasy in a Brooklyn loft . . . It all seemed too hipster steampunk to have terribly much credibility or longevity.

Well, I'm wrong (at least about the credibility – time will decide the rest). Behind the self-consciously funky right-on YouTube videos with their talk of sustainability, there is a seriousness of purpose, some real intellectual depth and a coherent philosophy. I guess that's what the folks at the Oxford Botanic Garden and the Ashmolean Museum saw when they were persuaded to lend their name to TOAD gins.

That credibility comes through in their first release, this Oxford Dry Gin. There is also a vodka, which I suppose we can forgive them as they do make their own base grain spirit and plan to produce whisky from the landrace cereal varieties grown for them by local archaeo-botanist John Letts. I've seen this work very well for Bruichladdich on Islay but it's challenging, as the grains can be demanding to work with and it requires a fundamental rethinking of the business model of distilling as we have come to understand it.

And that is why this distillery is in some ways more important than the products it makes. Their approach challenges current orthodoxy and insists that we can look at distilling holistically from grain to bottle. Setting up and running a small business is challenging enough and the life of a small-scale craft distiller isn't a bed of roses – to attempt it while at the same time defying industry norms requires either real courage or, more likely, a certain perversity of character and a wilful refusal to consider the stakes involved.

Either way, I hope you will support them. Visit the distillery, in agreeable Oxford; buy their gin (and possibly even the vodka for your less enlightened friends); and spread the word.

70

OXLEY

BRAND OWNER: Oxley Spirits Company
(Bacardi)

DISTILLERY: Oxley Spirits Company (Thames
Distillers Ltd for Bacardi)
Thames Distillers, Timbermill
Distillery, Clapham, London

WEBSITE: www.oxleygin.com

VISITOR CENTRE: Certainly not!

STRENGTH: 47%

OTHER VARIANTS: None

This rather beautifully packaged super-premium gin is actually a Bacardi product – not that you would know that from its low-profile approach. I wanted to see it being made, so I asked to visit the distillery. I enquired, politely I thought. Their marketing man recoiled in horror. 'That won't be possible.'

I like a challenge, so, just a few days later, I breezed nonchalantly onto a nondescript south London industrial estate sandwiched between a timber merchant and some rail tracks, trying hard not to be noticed (marketing men have spies everywhere). Once past an intimidating security barrier, had marketing man been watching, he would have seen two middle-aged chaps enter a large metal shed, which bore all the glamour of a run-down Northern carpet warehouse.

But appearances are not everything; for here I saw the Oxley Cold Distillation process. The still – unrecognisable as such – appears to be something from the laboratory of *Back to the Future* inventor Dr Emmett Brown. But from it flows slowly – excruciatingly slowly – a gin of sublime delicacy and refinement, so perfectly smooth, fresh, creamy and utterly mouth-watering that as I write this I am consuming a good tumblerful, neat and at room temperature. Bad Ian.

Vacuum distillation is not entirely unknown, but Oxley have combined this with a gizmo that forces the spirit vapour to hit a cold thingy (I promised not to reveal the technical secrets). And by 'cold' I mean *cold*. Colder than penguins' feet. Colder than an unimaginably cold thing on Planet Cold.

This means that the spirit retains all the delicacy and freshness of the botanicals, which include, most unusually, fresh grapefruit, orange and lemon. When you uncork the bottle you get a delicious burst of enticing citrus notes entreating you to 'drink me, drink me'. Apparently they had thirty-eight goes at the recipe. They got it right, if you ask me.

Don't worry if it looks expensive at around £50. It's a litre bottle of 47% deliciousness. Actually, they should charge more. That's not something I say very often, so hopefully the marketing man will forgive me now.

Sorry about visiting the distillery though.

71

PALMERS 44

BRAND OWNER: W. H. Palmer Group
DISTILLERY: The Langley Distillery, Langley
Green, Warley, West Midlands
WEBSITE: www.palmersgin.com
VISITOR CENTRE: No
STRENGTH: 44%
OTHER VARIANTS: None

This gin thing – it's all very new, right? Well, wrong, actually. Gin has been around and causing trouble for several centuries, but it is true that lots of the people making it and the brands they offer us are very new indeed. However, and it's an important however, even a new gin can have an old story. And so it proves here.

Unless you've been reading this book carefully you probably won't have heard of W. H. Palmer, the Langley distillery or their operating business Alcohols Ltd. But they make a number of the gins listed here and a great many more. If you have an idea for a new gin (cannabis-infused, perhaps) you take your concept and your chequebook to them and they will help you realise the dream. Then you have to package, sell and market it, which is when you realise it was really a nightmare. Anyway . . .

In its quiet and largely anonymous way, the Langley distillery has been serving the drinks industry since 1902 and Palmers themselves go back nearly a century prior to that. Over the years, they've collected quite an array of different shapes and sizes of stills, including the McKay which reputedly dates back to the mid-1800s. It's a curious fact that gin stills virtually never wear out – just their distillers.

However, for their first eponymous venture into marketing Palmers have elected to employ Angela, the family's copper pot which was built in 1903. Palmers 44 is, as you might expect, distilled following traditional gin distillation methods. The botanicals – juniper, coriander, angelica, cassia, liquorice, orris and grapefruit – are steeped overnight in 100% English wheat spirit while being warmed, allowing the botanicals to release their essential oils. It's a classic London Dry, shorn of any gimmicks, and can't fail to please the more traditional end of the market (like me).

But it does raise an interesting question, as Palmers claim to be responsible for distilling over 300 stock gin recipes as well as creating bespoke recipes for over 80% of the UK's artisanal brands. Can they serve two masters? Contract distilling is all very well, but trouble may lie ahead when you start to compete with your own customers. It will be interesting to see how this long-established firm of specialists will fare as they move outside their known area of expertise.

Whatever the outcome, though, this is a great start. Shame it's taken them over 200 years to get around to it!

72

PLYMOUTH

BRAND OWNER: Coates & Company
(Pernod Ricard)

DISTILLERY: Black Friars Distillery, Plymouth,
Devon

WEBSITE: www.plymouthgin.com

VISITOR CENTRE: Yes

STRENGTH: 41.2%

OTHER VARIANTS: Navy Strength, Sloe

Hello, sailor! Back in 1896, Plymouth Gin was specified in the earliest documented recipe for a Dry Martini (I expect you're shaken but not stirred). Despite the early fame, this grand old brand ended up as a makeweight in a series of corporate deals, passing from hand to hand through a series of uncomprehending and largely uncaring owners. It was probably too small and insignificant for anyone to even notice, and so escaped rationalisation and closure until eventually it came into the hands of Pernod Ricard. They own Beefeater and know and care about gin.

The interesting fact about Plymouth is that while London Gin can be produced anywhere (because it's a style), since a court action in the 1880s Plymouth has only been produced in the city itself. The legal action, against a number of London-based distillers who were selling 'Plymouth' gin, suggests the name itself had some cachet. (Note: if starting a new boutique distillery it might be an idea to do it there.) For some years the brand enjoyed Protected Geographical Origin status in EU law, but the relevant geographical indicator has now lapsed, though production remains firmly at the Black Friars distillery.

Due perhaps to the soft Dartmoor water, the Plymouth style is somewhat sweeter than the classic London Dry style, possessing deep earthy notes and a wonderfully fresh juniper and lemony bite. It has a slight sweetness due to the selection of botanicals with extraordinary concentration and complexity. No single botanical dominates the overall flavour.

Beloved of the Royal Navy, especially when served with Angostura bitters as the enduring Pink Gin, Plymouth Gin is now enjoying something of a revival (which is just as well as our Navy now seems to consist of not very much at all) in smarter cocktail bars and amongst gin drinkers looking for something a little offbeat but not so *outré* as might scandalise the vicar.

After its various vicissitudes, this famous old brand looks well settled in its new home and happy in its new packaging (I never really understood or liked the brief flirtation with the *faux*-Art Deco bottle which was neither stylish nor reflected Plymouth's heritage).

If your taste runs to a stronger tot, try Plymouth's Navy Strength (57%) – a right old howitzer amongst gins, very highly rated by aficionados and top cocktail barmen (OK, mixologists).

73

POLLINATION

BRAND OWNER: Dyfi Distillery Ltd

DISTILLERY: Dyfi, Corris, Machynlleth, Wales

WEBSITE: www.dyfidistillery.com

VISITOR CENTRE: Yes

STRENGTH: 45%

OTHER VARIANTS: Original, Hibernation

How green was my valley. Well, very green in the case of the Dyfi Valley on the southern edge of the Snowdonia National Park. So green, in fact, that UNESCO have designated it a 'World Biosphere Reserve', look you.

And in this special yet fragile place, brothers Pete and Danny Cameron forage rare local botanicals such as rowanberries, rosehips, sloes, hawthorn, elderflower, bog myrtle, bramble and birch leaves, meadowsweet, cicely, heather and lemon balm. There's juniper in there as well, along with lemon rind, liquorice and almonds from beyond the valley which combine with another baker's dozen of botanicals, pure spring water and British wheat spirit to make up Pollination – winner of the 2017 Great British Food Awards 'Best UK Gin'.

Having farmed, foraged and kept bees in Dyfi for more than thirty years, Pete knows this land well. His brother brings vital drinks business expertise with a connection to the port industry that enabled him to source an unusual white port cask in which to age their Hibernation gin. It's one of the better cask-aged gins that it's been my pleasure to try, but hurry up if you want one, because production is very, very limited.

That's true of everything they make, as theirs is a meticulous and demanding approach. Capacity is limited, not just by the size of the stills (two, of just 100 litres each, imported from Colorado and then customised) but by the need to hand forage the botanicals. If they can't be found, there can't be any distilling and Dyfi typically distils only once weekly. It's commercial madness, but a level of dedication and commitment that you just have to admire.

So, as you would expect, their gins are simply but beautifully packaged. Using a distinctive tall bottle, the label wraps round to virtually join up at the back. A montage of botanicals features a loosely drawn bee (naturally enough, on Pollination) and the top of the label is cut to shape to fit around the illustration. Each bottle is signed and dated by hand. They're quite lovely.

Pollination offers up a fresh and grassy nose with lavender and juniper notes that leads you naturally into the taste: spicy, slightly sweet and creamy with lots of body to carry tonic or stand out in your favourite cocktail. There's no slick corporate visitor centre but they do welcome curious and enthusiastic gin hunters and are happy to chat about what they do. It's the original welcome in the hillside.

PORTOBELLO ROAD

BRAND OWNER:	Leelex Ltd, Leeds, Yorkshire
DISTILLERY:	Thames Distillers, Timbermill Distillery, Clapham, London
WEBSITE:	www.portobelloroadgin.com
VISITOR CENTRE:	Yes (Ginstitute Museum)
STRENGTH:	42%
OTHER VARIANTS:	Navy Strength

With several hundred gin brands now on the market, and more arriving every week, it's genuinely hard to create something new that has the vital point of difference that will pull in drinkers – and that's if you can convince the notoriously hard-bitten trade buyers who are constantly being pitched new ideas. Which, of course, they take great relish in crushing with their renowned cynicism, world-class brutality and calculated cruelty (like publishers, with less charm).

So, for Portobello Road to have come up with a brand as recently as autumn 2011 that is already being stocked in at least one major supermarket is a considerable achievement; all the more so when in essence it came about accidentally. When proprietors Ged Feltham and Jake Burger were experimenting with (very) small-scale distilling for their Ginstitute Museum located above their Portobello Star pub this product took on a life of its own. And that is all the more remarkable when you consider that at that stage they were essentially pub and club operators and the museum was simply an idea to fill empty floors above the Portobello Star.

Today, the Ginstitute is the place to go in London to learn more about gin. Ged and Jake created it to hold their collection of vintage gins and to provide the opportunity for visitors to blend their own bespoke gin. To do that they needed a variety of distillates, which they prepared in their tiny Portuguese pot still (similar in style to the ones at 58 and Tarquin's) – but before long they had also created a classy London Dry with gin's long-time favourite botanicals joined, unusually, by nutmeg.

Cutting a long story short, that very soon found favour with buyers here and abroad, and production had to be turned over to Charles Maxwell at Thames Distillers who was able to scale up the quantities in his Tom Thumb still. However, it's not just the gin – excellent though it is – that stands out.

The bottle resembles a classic cognac bottle and the label, clearly designed with a great love of Victorian graphics, combines nostalgia with contemporary shelf appeal and visual impact. In a crowded market, nothing else looks quite like Portobello Road, and that is a very hard trick to pull off.

75

PYYGIN

BRAND OWNER: Teerenpeli Distillery Co.

DISTILLERY: Teerenpeli, Lahti, Finland

WEBSITE: www.teerenpelidistillery.com

VISITOR CENTRE: Yes – in restaurant

STRENGTH: 45%

OTHER VARIANTS: Wood Gin

Though relatively little known outside its native Finland, Teerenpeli has a great claim to being one of the earliest craft distilleries. Operations started in the basement of the family's Taivaanranta restaurant in Lahti in 2002 where, with the best of equipment and training from a well-known retired Scottish distiller, they started making malt whisky.

Being typically Finnish they were determined to do a good job, so nothing appeared on the market for at least seven years and – again this seems typically Finnish – they didn't make a great song and dance about it. But the whisky was excellent and deservedly developed a loyal following, with older releases and different cask finishes soon following. Before long, they had outgrown the original distillery, which as befits a true small-batch product is where the gin is now made.

A small brewery business was also established and, alongside it, space was created in 2015 for a new, enlarged whisky distillery modelled on the original plant. The gin craze also reached Finland and so PyyGin was born in September 2016 – the name comes from owner Anssi Pyysing, though the pun probably works better in Finnish.

What we have here is a tasty 45% expression, made in a proper pot still and using some interesting local botanicals including aroma hops, birch leaves and lingonberries. The nose combines plenty of juniper to please traditionalists, with wafts of enticing citrus. It's very pleasant and easy to drink neat, if that is your preference, but works really well in a classic gin and tonic as it has the body and weight to let the gin sing through without overly dominating the mix.

This is a very well-mannered gin from a firmly established small distiller. Finland may be a somewhat unexpected source of great spirits but there is a fast-growing and vibrant distilling community there doing great work – see also the entries for Helsinki and Napue gins, both excellent.

Teerenpeli also make a more experimental wood-finished version, which is notably spicier and markedly drier – definitely one for sipping. One of my favourite words in Finnish (don't you have one?) is *nousuhumala*, which describes the feeling of getting pleasantly drunk at the start of the evening. PyyGin really hits the spot for a pre-prandial G&T yet the wood-aged version, sipped to the accompaniment of Sibelius's moody and magnificent *The Wood Nymph*, might better suit the piece's somewhat arboreal ambience. *Kippis!*

76

ROCK ROSE

BRAND OWNER: Dunnet Bay Distillers Ltd,
Thurso, Caithness

DISTILLERY: Dunnet Bay, Thurso, Caithness

WEBSITE: www.dunnetbaydistillers.co.uk

VISITOR CENTRE: Yes

STRENGTH: 41.5%

OTHER VARIANTS: Navy Strength

ROCK ROSE

HAND CRAFTED SCOTTISH GIN

OUR PRECIOUS BOTANICALS ARE BLESSED WITH THE FRESHEST AIR AND PUREST
HIGHLAND WATER. THEY ARE LOVINGLY PREPARED BEFORE BEING HAND-DISTILLED
TO CREATE A TRUE TASTE OF OUR BEAUTIFUL AND RUGGED COASTLINE.

**SCOTTISH
BOTANICALS**

Flavourful and fresh, zesty yet berryful
with a long smooth finish.
One of nature's little treats.

Here's a truly hand-crafted Scottish gin that, in just its first few weeks, achieved quite a splash of attention and made a healthy start on the goal to sell 10,000 bottles a year (that's a lot for a small, start-up operation). What's more, it's in about as remote a location as you can imagine anywhere in mainland Britain and, while setting it up, co-founder Martin Murray spent around half his time on an oil rig in the North Sea where he worked as a process engineer.

That's a big part of the success. Having qualified at Heriot-Watt University, Martin and wife Claire longed to return home to Caithness and set up their own brewing and distilling business. So Martin obtained further experience with the university's School of Brewing and Distilling and, after a lot of research and trials, was able to set up his own Dunnet Bay distillery in late 2014.

The still was manufactured to a unique design by John Dore & Company and features an unusual stainless-steel body with a copper dome and column; the result is efficient heating, combined with lots of copper contact in the condensing phase – so important to flavour in the spirit. All the botanicals are contained in a separate Carterhead-style basket to preserve the delicacy of the locally sourced ingredients.

They too are a little unusual: as well as the regulation juniper and the more conventional cardamom, Martin and Claire are using rose root, sea buckthorn, rowan (keeps away the witches, as we know) and blaeberries. The result of these, and a few secret others, together with long, slow distillation and vapour infusion, is a light, fragrant and floral gin with a most attractive and distinctive nose that doesn't lack for body or mouthfeel.

A small business such as this has an inbuilt advantage at the capital investment stage as it can qualify for substantial grants from Scotland's enterprise agencies (as this did). But it still requires great personal commitment of time and money (well over £100,000 in this case) and the challenges of the remote location never go away. I checked, and the distillery is more than 270 miles (over six hours' hard driving) from Edinburgh's Bramble Bar, a great gin joint.

If ever you make it to John O'Groats, take the time to visit the distillery: their Rock Rose gin is a very fine product indeed, one that speaks volumes about what can be achieved with talent, energy and some lovely local botanicals.

77

ROKU

BRAND OWNER: Suntory Holdings Ltd

DISTILLERY: Yamazaki, Osaka, Japan

WEBSITE: https://www.suntory.co.jp/wnb/
rokugin/en/

VISITOR CENTRE: Yes

STRENGTH: 43% (47% in Japan)

OTHER VARIANTS: None

You wait for ages and three come along at once. Buses in the rain? No, Japanese gins. Virtually no gin having been distilled in Japan in living memory, we now have three to compare. That's gin made in Japan, because there are Japanese-inspired gins made in the UK but, as we're being a bit purist here, they don't count.

You could say that I should get out more, but the thing is they are very well made, very good and they bring some real variety to the more-or-less standard botanicals that appear more-or-less everywhere. And, even more excitement, they're really quite different from each other.

This Roku, for example, comes from the giant Suntory group which is Japan's largest distiller and now a global force in the spirits industry. It's made in the grandly named 'Liquor Atelier', a separate operation within the Yamazaki Distillery in Osaka; in effect a specialised craft distillery for Suntory's more unusual spirits and liquor. Without slipping too far into cliché or national stereotypes, it's made with a distinctly Japanese attention to detail that is close to obsessive.

For example, four different types of pot still are used to distil the fourteen botanicals separately, according to the nature of each, as the distillery seeks to extract the best flavour while maintaining their individual characteristics. The delicate cherry blossom is prepared in a stainless-steel pot still (a most unusual vessel) under vacuum where other, more robust botanicals are distilled in copper.

The botanicals are carefully selected: eight traditional varieties for an authentic gin taste and six Japanese botanicals cultivated over four seasons and harvested at their peak to add a distinctive Japanese twist to the final blend. The search for perfection continues into the packaging, which is a thing of beauty. Naturally the bottle features six facets to reflect the six Japanese botanicals (*roku* is Japanese for 'six'), and the label design and even the paper have been selected to further highlight Japanese craftsmanship and sentiment. The whole ensemble works elegantly together and is harmonious and graceful.

Naturally, there is a recommended serve and even a special Roku measuring cup – it's suggested that you dispense 5cl (basically a double) directly into a pre-poured glass of ice and tonic, garnished with strips of fresh ginger. It's not what you expect, but isn't that exactly the point? Moreover, it's excellent. *Kampai!*

78

SACRED

BRAND OWNER:	Sacred Spirits Company Ltd
DISTILLERY:	Sacred, Highgate, London
WEBSITE:	www.sacredspiritscompany.com
VISITOR CENTRE:	No (private house)
STRENGTH:	40%
OTHER VARIANTS:	Christmas Pudding, Pink Grapefruit, Cardamom, Juniper, Negroni Giftpack, Gin Blending Kit

Imagine if you will, gin as a work of art, something that the Tate Gallery might exhibit. No need – it exists. But this is an exhibit that you get to consume – making you, you might say, part of the artwork itself. Or, to be strictly accurate, you could until it ran out – that's the problem with limited editions. Perhaps it's now a conceptual artwork.

But, if the idea appeals, you can actually become the artist yourself, creating your own utterly unique bespoke gin with Sacred's Gin Blending Kit. One of the very first micro-distilling operations, Sacred now makes around 1,000 bottles a week – not bad for a distillery established in 2009 that operates from a room in a private house in North London. That must have been an interesting conversation with the neighbours.

Joint owner and distiller Ian Hart is another refugee from the City, who turned to distilling when the financial world broke bad: perhaps he, Daniel Szor (Cotswold), Robin Gerlach (Elephant) and Victoria Christie (Graveney) should form an escape committee to persuade more of their former colleagues to join them. Fewer bankers and more distillers, that's the recipe for greater Gross National Happiness.

Actually, Sacred does in many ways exemplify the GNH approach to life. Everything is produced by hand on their table-top, low-pressure cold vacuum-distilling apparatus – a rotary evaporator to the technically minded. Nothing is rushed: the twelve botanicals at the heart of Sacred's gins are all macerated for up to a month and a half before being distilled separately then blended to individual recipes and bottled at 40%.

Not so very long ago the idea of cold distilling under a vacuum seemed eccentric and doomed to failure. But the quality of Sacred's products soon convinced bartenders that here was something special and others took note.

Apart from the capital cost, the huge benefit of cold distillation is that it maintains the freshness and vibrancy of the more delicate botanicals, something that is a signature note in Sacred's products. With his meticulous small-batch approach and insistence on hands-on production Ian Hart is not going to conquer the world of gin but he has the satisfaction of having changed it.

His are landmark products that every gin lover should try.

79

SAFFRON

BRAND OWNER: Gabriel Boudier

DISTILLERY: Boudier, Dijon, France

WEBSITE: www.boudier.com

VISITOR CENTRE: No

STRENGTH: 40%

OTHER VARIANTS: Rare London Dry

You probably know Gabriel Boudier for their Crème de Cassis de Dijon – a product so highly esteemed they were awarded the Légion d'honneur, France's highest decoration. Think of it as the nearest thing to a republican Royal Warrant and you'll get the idea.

They have been making their liqueurs since 1874 so they know a thing or two about distilling. The company is still family owned and distinctively French in style – something expressed wonderfully well in their ornate labels. Saffron Gin's label is quite restrained by their standards but, delightfully, is actually printed on tin, not paper, an idiosyncratic touch that I greatly appreciated. But that, of course, is not what you first notice about this gin …

Yes, it's the colour – uncomfortably close to a glass of Irn-Bru, not that that distinctively Scottish beverage is frequently poured in Dijon, or indeed in the sophisticated cocktail bars that are the natural habitat of this product. The colour is derived from saffron, reputedly the most expensive of spices and one that was apparently used in the nineteenth century in a recipe discovered in the Boudier archive. Though we think of India during this period as a British colony, there were French outposts in Pondicherry, Chandernagor and Madras, and Indian spices were imported to Europe where they would have found their way into gin.

Whether because of cost or because it doesn't seem to me at least to sit well in gin, saffron never really established a place as a key botanical and isn't much used today. Diplôme and Cadenhead's Old Raj Gin, with their pale straw colour, are the only other ones that come to mind. Other than that, the botanicals in Boudier's version are fairly conventional: juniper, coriander, lemon, orange peel, angelica seeds, iris and fennel all feature. The saffron is added after distillation, making this a distilled gin probably best enjoyed in a cocktail (a Negroni, with its orange twist, works rather well).

Saffron Gin, despite its distinguished producer, is something of an outlier. Its colour marks it out from other gins and will offend the purist. It doesn't feel that well balanced to me, and the saffron tends to dominate and mask the other flavours. It's certainly one to try, however, but probably more as an occasional novelty rather than forming part of your established drinking repertoire.

80

SANTAMANÍA

BRAND OWNER: Unique Spirits SL

DISTILLERY: Santamanía Urban Distillery, Las Rozas, Madrid, Spain

WEBSITE: www.destileriaurbana.com

VISITOR CENTRE: No

STRENGTH: 41%

OTHER VARIANTS: Reserva, Legend Urban, Four Pillars

Here's something really quite unusual – a craft Spanish gin distillery, right in Madrid. Given the Spanish enthusiasm for gin, the skill and care with which it is served there and the massive range of brands you can find in almost any bar, you would assume that there are several small distilleries that have opened up to capitalise on this fantastic market, full of discriminating consumers.

Not so. In fact, as I write, this is Spain's only boutique gin distillery – think of it as a Sipsmith's and you'll begin to understand its importance. Santamanía in Spanish apparently suggests an obsessive attention to detail: well, the founders of this operation have certainly exhibited that.

To get started they had to argue over regulations and permissions for more than a year; they only ever make a maximum of 330 bottles at a time, but generally far fewer; they use grape spirit as their base and source unusual Spanish botanicals to give a distinctive twist to the final product.

The distilling process is a painstaking and labour-intensive one, involving twenty-four hours of maceration for the more robust botanicals, a full charge of their custom-built 280-litre Christian Carl still, use of a botanicals basket in a vapour chamber for the more delicate botanicals, a six-plate rectification column and then reduction with water brought specially from a Canary Islands volcano! After which the spirit rests for between two to three months before bottling. Every batch is individually identified and given a unique name and identity – these, maintain the distillers, are works of art.

Certainly the packaging stands apart, with a distinctive tall bottle with a funky red base that's covered in tiny etched detail – great fun to try to decode. First impressions on the nose are of red cherries, then liquorice root and a classic juniper bite. In total, fourteen botanicals are used, comprising juniper berries, coriander seed, liquorice root, fresh Spanish lime and lemon, angelica, orris root, Spanish pistachio nuts, raspberries, cinnamon, white pepper, dry ginger, rosemary, and, of course, those cherries. Quite a number of experimental batches were created before arriving at the final recipe, which, for such a young distillery, delivers an impressively mature and sophisticated product.

So, say 'hola!' to Santamanía, a Spanish gin that will shortly be popping up in great cocktail bars and collecting an impressive and well-deserved medal haul.

81

SHARISH BLUE MAGIC

BRAND OWNER: António Cuco

DISTILLERY: Sharish Distillery, Reguengos de Monsaraz, Portugal

WEBSITE: www.sharishgin.com

VISITOR CENTRE: www.sharishgin.com

STRENGTH: 40%

OTHER VARIANTS: Original, Laurinius, Pera Rocha

Talk about an overnight success. Less than five years ago, António Cuco was an unemployed tourism teacher, occasionally helping out at his parents' restaurant. He thought he might distil his own gin, so cut a hole in an old pressure cooker for a still and linked it via some coiled copper piping to an empty 10-litre plastic container that had previously held olive oil – as you might do if you aren't unduly concerned about blowing yourself up or hosting an unwelcome visit from Mr Plod (or whatever they call the constabulary in Portugal).

By 2014 he had acquired a qualification in distilling and, perhaps more importantly, two 300-litre stills lovingly nicknamed 'The Minions' (it's a change from ladies' names). Sharish Original was followed by the sensation that is Blue Magic – a deep blue gin that changes colour when tonic is added. It's a science thing: apparently the extract of flowers from the blue pea (*Clitoria ternatea*) react to the citric acid in tonic causing the colour to flush purple or pink, depending how much tonic you put in.

It's an extremely dramatic and unexpected effect that adds to the theatre of serving a G&T in the giant goblets so beloved of bars in the Iberian peninsula. Unfortunately, we didn't get off to the best of starts with this, Mrs B. observing that the gin itself 'looks like methylated spirits' (which she doesn't drink). However, I thought it was great fun and the market seems to agree as Sharish have gone from strength to strength, first in Portugal and then in export markets. A few imitators have piled in, and even good old Marks & Spencer now offer a colour-changing gin.

However, this was, I think, the first with the effect, and the presentation also stands out on shelf, being reminiscent of a bottle of Mateus Rosé and with a distinctive cut-out label featuring a profile of the medieval Templar castle of Monsaraz. Be aware, though, that it's a 50cl bottle which pushes the standard bottle equivalent typical UK retail price to over £50.

Original is, as the name suggests, the first Sharish gin; Laurinius is cask-aged for a year to add a gentle depth and richness to the flavour; and Pera Rocha is a limited-edition style using a pear variety native to Portugal. Now, in the words of that classic interview question, answer this: 'Where do you see *yourself* in five years' time?'

82

SHED 1 CUCKOLD'S REVENGE

BRAND OWNER:	Shed 1 Distillery Ulverston Ltd
DISTILLERY:	Shed 1, Ulverston, Cumbria
WEBSITE:	www.shed1distillery.com
VISITOR CENTRE:	No
STRENGTH:	44%
OTHER VARIANTS:	Giggle in the Ginnel, Fancy Frolic, limited seasonal releases

The Shed. What does that call to mind? The Fulham Road End stand at Chelsea FC? Or the Shed at Dulwich, perhaps, the infamous London restaurant that was top rated on TripAdvisor yet never actually existed? Or is 'the shed' for you the ultimate man cave – a sanctuary where you can listen to the Test Match in peace (is it just me, or are Test Matches best enjoyed on the wireless?) while contemplating the finer details of your next project?

Wouldn't a distillery be the ultimate man-cave shed project? Actually, there are now several 'Shed' distilleries. One in Ireland aims to produce 200,000 cases of various spirits each year and employ ten staff – not so much a shed as a small warehouse, then. There's a £6m project to create whisky in an Edinburgh Engine Shed – nice try. And there's one in Scotland, at Inshriach, which was making gin – it won Shed of the Year in 2015 – until they discovered they didn't actually have planning permission. That's embarrassing.

But Shed 1 in Ulverston takes the prize because it really is in a shed. A very small one – judging by the pictures – called Shed 1, because the owners have two and it clearly wouldn't do to get them mixed up. This is real small-batch distilling: they make just thirty-six of their half-litre bottles per run – that's about twenty-five standard bottles but, as they say, it's 'big flavoured gin . . . smooth enough to be sipped, bold enough to be mixed'.

That's a pretty fair ambition for any distiller. Can it deliver? Cuckold's Revenge is certainly smooth, with a beguiling nose and initial taste that opens nicely with beautifully balanced spice and citrus notes and a sweet liquorice finish. I'd grant it big flavour, while still being recognisably a gin.

The unusual name is a reference to Master Ford in Shakespeare's *Merry Wives of Windsor* (sorry, but as you may have noticed I'm a sucker for a literary reference), a character played by Shed 1's Andy Arnold-Bennett who, before distilling, was an actor. Speaking to Sir John Falstaff (Act 2, Scene 2, as if you cared) he's heard to say, 'There is money; spend it, spend it; spend more; spend all I have . . .'

That sounds just like setting up a small distillery, so let us trust that this is not a case of *Love's Labours Lost*, not a *Comedy of Errors* and that eventually *All's Well That Ends Well*!

SHORTCROSS

BRAND OWNER: Rademon Estate Distillery Ltd

DISTILLERY: Rademon Estate Distillery, Downpatrick

WEBSITE: www.shortcrossgin.com

VISITOR CENTRE: Yes

STRENGTH: 46%

OTHER VARIANTS: None

First impressions really count, and ShortCross have done exceptionally well here. Despite using a fairly dull standard bottle, the label is outstanding. The use of letterpress printing (I'm always a sucker for a nice piece of letterpress printing), the carefully selected typefaces and subtle use of foiling on the label, not to mention the clever way the batch number is hidden on the reverse, means you can happily spend some time exploring the label before even thinking of opening the bottle. That may sound as if I need to get out more, but there's no denying the appeal of a satisfyingly tactile and well-designed piece of packaging. I was half sold on ShortCross before I tasted it; everything about the presentation told me that this gin had been made by people who cared, and naturally I expected that to be reflected in a quality product.

That's where the problem started. ShortCross have chosen to seal the bottle with a heavy black wax: it looks great, but took me as long to get off as I had spent savouring the label. These wax seals are the very devil to remove. You end up hacking at them with a knife, placing your fingers in considerable peril of being sliced off and generally end up with little bits of wax all over the place.

But it was worth it in the end. Though novice distillers, owners Fiona and David Boyd-Armstrong have gone to considerable pains to create something rather special for what is Northern Ireland's first boutique gin, and they've set the bar high. Apart from the lovely label (did I mention that?), the care and long planning is apparent in their choice of equipment.

Quite a number of small distillers use stills from Carl of Germany. Few have gone for a 450-litre copper pot still linked to two enrichment columns, each with seven individual bubble plates. It's a fine-looking piece of equipment that permits close control of the reflux during distillation, contributing to the delivery of a very smooth yet characterful spirit. With this particular design, ShortCross will have the flexibility to produce a number of alternative products, so expect further gin and doubtless a vodka before long.

The Boyd-Armstrongs wanted to create a gin that reflected its provenance, hence the foraged wild clover and homegrown green apples. There are elderflowers and elderberries also in the botanicals: the result is sweet but not cloying, with a satisfyingly spicy and herbal finish.

84

SILENT POOL

BRAND OWNER:	The Surrey Hills Distilling Company Ltd
DISTILLERY:	Silent Pool Distillery, Albury, Surrey
WEBSITE:	www.silentpooldistillers.com
VISITOR CENTRE:	Yes
STRENGTH:	43%
OTHER VARIANTS:	Admiral Collingwood Navy Strength, English Rose

By contrast with the youthful team one has come to expect at a 'craft' distillery, Silent Pool can field a team of grizzled veterans. It includes two highly qualified distillers (both MSc graduates of the renowned Heriot-Watt University distilling course), a commercially very experienced veteran of the UK drinks distribution scene and a couple of seasoned business executives with many years' experience who remain discreetly in the shadows.

And despite being one of the newer operations mentioned here it's clear that they know exactly what they are doing. An impressive Arnold Holstein copper pot still with a seven-plate rectifying column and 'gin head' has been commissioned, allowing huge variation in creating different spirits (plans include whisky, vodka and liqueurs). Interestingly, the still itself is powered by steam from a wood-fired boiler.

The location, in a renovated barn on the Duke of Northumberland's Albury Estate, is most attractive. The name comes from a local beauty spot, the Silent Pool, part of the Surrey Hills Area of Outstanding Natural Beauty. The pool itself, from which the distillery will draw water, is said to be sacred, linked to a thirteenth-century legend of a beautiful young woodcutter's daughter who would bathe in the pure, clear waters. One day a nobleman rode by and, overcome by her beauty, moved towards her (the beast!). But rather than give in to his advances, she waded deeper into the water and drowned. Her father recognised the man as King John and to this day locals claim that the girl can still be spotted at the Silent Pool at midnight.

Well, I'm convinced. You won't catch me there, beautiful girl or not.

Silent Pool's original Master Distiller was Cory Mason, an American who has worked in top bars and craft distilling in the USA for more than fifteen years. He created an innovative distilling regime for Silent Pool and sourced a number of interesting botanicals, including locally grown kaffir limes, pear and honey. Today he can be found in Oxford (see entry 69) but he has left an impressive legacy.

With their strong industry credentials and attractive packaging, I expected in the first edition that Silent Pool would achieve rapid distribution in the best cocktail bars. Well, my confidence was well placed – they have made quite a splash and, unlike the legendary local lovely, seem to be swimming strongly to an island of profit.

85

SIPSMITH

BRAND OWNER: Beam Suntory Inc.

DISTILLERY: Sipsmith Distillery, Chiswick, London

WEBSITE: www.sipsmith.com

VISITOR CENTRE: Yes

STRENGTH: 41.6%

OTHER VARIANTS: Very Juniper Over Proof (VJOP), Lemon Drizzle, Sloe

First there was Bombay, then Hendrick's, but if any one single brand can be said to have kick-started boutique craft gin distillation in the UK it is Sipsmith. Not, of course, that they intended to do that, but the purposefully wacky guys wrote the book on small-batch, hand-crafted, artisanal, authentic – all the adjectives, in fact, beloved of the latest generation of distillers.

Their story begins in January 2007 when two old friends, Fairfax Hall and Sam Galsworthy, quit their jobs, sold their respective houses and determined to actually create the distillery they'd been talking about for the last five years. Very soon, by a remarkable set of improbable coincidences, they found a suitable property (formerly used by the late great Michael Jackson as a tasting room) that had once even been a micro-brewery. It then took two years of 'discussion' with HM Revenue & Customs to obtain a distilling licence – for which perseverance, every subsequent small distiller should give thanks, daily.

Drinks writer Jared Brown joined them as distiller and mastered the fine intricacies of Prudence, their original Christian Carl still. The bespoke design, combining a pot with a Carterhead and a column, makes for incredible versatility and allows the distillation of both vodka and gin from one apparatus. The first production was in March 2009 and initial deliveries were made by hand, using Galsworthy's moped! Order after order followed, as gin took hold of the imagination of London's mixologists and their customers; less than a year later major supermarkets and off-licences were stocking the brand and very soon afterwards a second still, Patience, was installed.

Several other expressions, including the mighty VJOP, have followed; and, more recently, a move to enlarged premises in Chiswick with further distillation capacity in the form of Constance, their third still. Then, of course, the big boys came calling, and in December 2016 Sipsmith was bought by Beam Suntory. The partners, still all active in the business, are rightly proud of what has been achieved but are coy on the purchase price – £50 million has been suggested, though.

Sipsmith has achieved incredible growth in a very short time and is something of a poster boy for the craft distilling movement. While inspiring many others to follow in their footsteps, few will be quite as successful, or as well rewarded, but if they have half the fun and make gin half as good their life will be an exciting one.

86

SLINGSBY

BRAND OWNER:	Spirit of Harrogate Ltd
DISTILLERY:	The Langley Distillery, Langley Green, Warley, West Midlands
WEBSITE:	www.wslingsby.co.uk
VISITOR CENTRE:	Yes, at 5–7 Montpellier Parade, Harrogate
STRENGTH:	42%
OTHER VARIANTS:	Rhubarb, Navy Strength, Barrel Aged

There's a lot of the locality in Slingsby – seventeen of its twenty-four botanicals have been grown in Harrogate's Rudding Park Hotel kitchen garden and the name itself honours local worthy William Slingsby who first discovered the restorative powers of the local waters back in 1571 – but the gin itself is distilled by our old friends at the Langley distillery.

But, to be fair, Slingsby are quite transparent about that and the energetic chaps behind the brand still supply pre-mixed botanical packs to Langley and the spirit is reduced to bottling strength with water from Harrogate's Tewit Well, the original Slingsby's claim to fame. So, all in all, I believe we can accept their claim to be the 'spirit of Harrogate', which is what they have styled their 'visitor experience' in the town's smart Montpellier Parade. In fact, so successful has this been that what was intended as a short-lived pop-up has now taken on permanent form and is available for tastings and private events, as well as the obvious opportunity for retail therapy.

Slingsby was launched as recently as August 2015, after an eighteen-month development period, making it something of a veteran in today's market, but seems to be sticking around. It certainly has a local fan club, as I discovered at a tasting I held as part of the Harrogate Book Festival in October 2017. There was supposed to be a bottle left over for me at the end, but between the enthusiasm of the audience and a 'misunderstanding' by the lovely volunteers on the event team it had mysteriously evaporated by the time I left the stage (only after extended rapturous applause, may I add).

But don't be alarmed on my account, as I have tried it since and can give a favourable report on this sweet and citrus-forward drop of Yorkshire goodness. The house serve suggests a pink grapefruit twist and blueberry garnish and this certainly complements the fruity notes in the gin. But coming through on the finish is rhubarb, always a welcome tasting note.

Perhaps this, or perhaps it was their proximity to the famous Rhubarb Triangle that inspired Slingsby to create their own Yorkshire Rhubarb Gin which tastes, funnily enough, of rhubarb. But it has proved a superb twist on traditional gins and there are now several rhubarb gins on offer. Few will match this.

Incidentally, rhubarb is a vegetable not a fruit. The things you learn . . .

87

SLOANE'S

BRAND OWNER: Toorank Distilleries BV,
Zevenaar, The Netherlands

DISTILLERY: Toorank, Zevenaar,
The Netherlands

WEBSITE: www.sloanes-gin.com

VISITOR CENTRE: No

STRENGTH: 40%

OTHER VARIANTS: None

Sloane's: you would imagine, wouldn't you, that the name is a reference to the Sloane Ranger, the archetypal upper-class Londoner whose self-possessed, braying tones one could quite convincingly imagine ordering a large G&T with all the confidence and privilege associated with the label (if you're reading this in the USA, think 'preppy'). But you'd be wrong.

The serious-minded Dutch distillers had another Londoner in mind: inspired by Sir Hans Sloane's (1660–1753) personal botanical collection which formed the foundation of the British and Natural History Museum collections.

We can't of course be sure, and (being a gentleman) Sloane does not appear to have any documented connection to the gin trade, but it is suggested by Toorank that Sloane's botanicals introduced to the UK a number of then exotic ingredients such as juniper berries, fresh oranges and lemons, orris root, angelica, cardamom, coriander, cassia bark, liquorice and vanilla. These, of course, have formed the basis for creating gins ever since. It's a pleasing theory, even if the historical evidence may be lacking. After all, London's Worshipful Company of Distillers was founded more than twenty years before Sloane was born and published *The Distiller of London*, a book of rules and instructions, as early as 1638.

Toorank are actually a large contract distiller, producing third-party products, as well as their own brands. They set some bold objectives for Sloane's and have gone about distilling it in a particularly meticulous way. Using a relatively small still, each of the ten botanicals is distilled separately, left to rest for between two to three months before being blended together and then rested again, prior to bottling. They use only fresh fruit, rather than peel, evident in the marked citrus note and clean fresh nose.

Shortly after it launched, Sloane's was awarded World's Best Gin and Best White Spirit, and was a Double Gold Medal winner at the San Francisco World Spirit Competition in 2011. As far as I can determine, it hasn't been placed at any major awards subsequently, but the company may have decided to rest on their laurels for a while as this led to an unexpected and hard-to-manage surge in demand.

It's well worth tracking down – just try to ask for it nicely, yah.

88

ST. GEORGE TERROIR

BRAND OWNER: St. George Spirits

DISTILLERY: St. George Spirits, Alameda, California, USA

WEBSITE: www.stgeorgespirits.com

VISITOR CENTRE: Distillery tours available

STRENGTH: 45%

OTHER VARIANTS: Botanivore, Dry Rye Gin

Wow! Just, wow! The first time I tasted this it absolutely took my breath away, such is the unexpected nature of the taste and the explosive impact of the first sip. And it was just as remarkable on the second and subsequent occasions. In fact, I think I can say that out of all the gins that I tasted for this book this was the one that lingered longest and I could recall most distinctly the next day.

That's not always a good thing, however. I can think of one or two that were memorable for all the wrong reasons (they didn't make the cut, needless to say), but, while this is a love-it-or-hate-it kind of a spirit, it's clearly made with a point of view. Or perhaps attitude would be more apt, for this hails from the St. George Spirits distillery in Alameda, California, arguably the birthplace of the modern American artisan distillation movement. This was founded in 1982 by Jörg Rupf, a German immigrant with family connections to the distilling of fruit spirits in the Black Forest. He established a small distillery to recreate the products he remembered from Germany and, in the process, changed everything that was then known about distilling in the USA.

Several other very well-known artisan distillers in the USA trained here and have gone on to establish their own operations, often with considerable success. And St George's, now owned by Lance Winters, has grown to the point where it now occupies a 65,000-square-feet building and operates a number of stills, making a full range of spirits.

They describe Terroir as 'inspired by the forests of Northern California' and suggest that 'the taste will transport you somewhere beautiful and wild'. Included in the botanicals are Douglas fir, California bay laurel and coastal sage along with nine other more conventional botanicals. They distil the fir and sage individually in a 250-litre still to minimise the impact of seasonal variation, while the fresh bay laurel leaves and juniper berries are vapour infused in a botanicals basket and the other botanicals go right into their 1,500-litre pot still. The result is a walk in the pinewoods.

It's remarkable. Whether this can truly be called gin is debatable. I doubt most gin drinkers would find it acceptable but I will admit that I went back to the glass time after time, if only to confirm that I hadn't imagined its dramatic, intense aromas and taste.

In fact, I'm pining for it now.

89

STRANE MERCHANT STRENGTH

BRAND OWNER:	Smögen Whisky AB
DISTILLERY:	Smögen Whisky AB, Hunnebostrand, Sweden
WEBSITE:	www.strane.se
VISITOR CENTRE:	Distillery tours available by appointment
STRENGTH:	47.4%
OTHER VARIANTS:	Navy Strength, Uncut

Gin? From a whisky distillery? In Sweden? Yes, it's all true. Smögen Whisky was established in 2010 by lawyer and whisky author turned distiller Pär Caldenby and has proved one of the success stories of Swedish craft distilling (there have been failures).

They make three gins, all in small quantities, in a tiny 100-litre wood-fired pot still. True to their whisky roots, blending is at the heart of what they do, and the production process at Strane is both interesting and unusual. Actually, Hendrick's does something similar and, curious but true, that's also made by a company better known for its whisky.

Beginning with the same twelve botanicals (juniper, coriander, sage, lime and lemon peel, basil, mint, sweet almond, cinnamon, liquorice and two secret ingredients native to Sweden) Caldenby uses them to create three separate distillates with distinct flavours. The separate distillates – not finished gins at this stage – one juniper-y, the second citrus dominated and the third more herbal are then blended in different ratios to create three final products. Simples! Whisky blenders do this all the time, except they use the products of different distilleries and varying cask types.

The thinking behind this is to emphasise and consistently deliver the flavour of each group of botanicals, exploiting the fact that different botanicals behave differently at different boiling points. Rather than adopting a 'one size fits all' approach, this allows the team scope to explore the subtler notes in each.

The base spirits are then blended to produce the three expressions, Merchant, Navy and Uncut – all are bottled at different strengths and quite distinctive in style and flavour. Of course the key to product consistency then lies in the blending, exactly like a blended Scotch whisky. The first and most widely available is their Merchant Strength, itself a chunky 47.4% bruiser; the Uncut reaches an alarming 75.3% abv – it's not for the unwary!

Gin made like this, at a higher strength, in small batches, in a high-wage economy such as Sweden's, is never going to be cheap. You'll find Strane in a few UK specialists at around £40 for their 50cl bottle (the equivalent of £56 for a standard bottle), which pushes it into super-premium territory. So it's probably more of a special treat than an everyday tipple, unless those secret Swedish botanicals really float your boat.

90

STRATHEARN SCOTTISH DRY

BRAND OWNER: Strathearn Distillery Ltd

DISTILLERY: Strathearn Distillery, Bachilton Farm Steading, Methven, Perth

WEBSITE: www.strathearndistillery.com

VISITOR CENTRE: Yes – by appointment

STRENGTH: 47%

OTHER VARIANTS: Heather Rose, Oaked, Citrus

Claiming to be 'probably Scotland's smallest distillery', Strathearn was opened in August 2013, and despite its size punches well above its weight. It has had a powerful and positive influence on the Scottish craft distilling scene.

Founder Tony Reeman-Clark played a formative role in establishing the Scottish Craft Distillers Association, which works to encourage growth within the sector and defend the authenticity of Scottish craft spirits (incidentally, something similar is badly needed for England and Wales). With their artisanal Portuguese stills from Hoga they have also mentored many aspiring distillers who have gone on to establish their own small distillery. If that's your dream you could do worse than try their five-day Whisky Making School to gain hands-on experience of artisan distilling (I daresay that you could ask them for a few gin tips). Or invest just one day of the rest of your life in a Gin Making Experience – the best £145 you'll spend in a long time.

Strathearn make on a true small-batch basis, producing just 280 bottles of their signature Strathearn Scottish Dry gin at one time. Even at that, the spirit is a combination of gin from their two stills, one of 500-litres capacity (small) and one 50-litres (tiny), which is, they say, 'distilled with passion, crafted with skill and bottled with pride'.

It's certainly old school. Bottled at a useful 47%, it is definitely a juniper-led gin with plenty of slightly sweet pine notes, which are soon overtaken by pepper and lemon verbena sherbet. The botanical list is simple but intriguing: juniper, coriander seeds, angelica root, orris root, grains of paradise, orange peel and rose petals are conventional enough, but calamus root and honeyberry add an unusual touch. Traditionalists amongst the gin-drinking fraternity will love this. Like the distillery itself, this seems to play in a higher league.

But if Scottish Dry is too much gin for you then splash your tonic of choice into their Heather Rose and watch it do that colour-changing trick that's been so successful for Sharish, but with Scottish heather emphasising its Perthshire credentials. Oaked Highland is more of a sipping gin – 'where whisky meets gin' they say – and Citrus adds Italian lemons and Spanish grapefruit with a suggestion of kaffir lime leaves and star anise, very much designed for cocktails or long-mixing.

So, lots to see and do at Strathearn; very definitely a shining light on the Scottish distilling scene.

91

TANQUERAY TEN

BRAND OWNER: Diageo plc

DISTILLERY: Cameronbridge, Fife

WEBSITE: www.tanqueray.com

VISITOR CENTRE: No

STRENGTH: 47.3%

OTHER VARIANTS: Export Strength, Rangpur,
Flor de Sevilla

Here's proof – if proof were needed – that big brands can be cool, sexy and very, very good. Because this super-premium expression of one of the USA's favourite gins is all those things: it's what's in the bottle that counts, and here we have a gin that any distiller would be proud to offer up, any fashionable cocktail watering hole happy to mix and any discerning drinker more than content to savour.

Tanqueray started life in London in 1830 but has had an itinerant existence since the war. It now seems settled in its own dedicated gin hall located within Diageo's giant Cameronbridge distilling complex – unfortunately, so large and busy is the site it seems unlikely that public access will ever be possible. Never mind, I popped in to take a look for you and I can report it is both hugely impressive and reassuringly calm.

The venerable Old Tom No. 4a still and its diminutive fellow Tiny Tim both seem well settled in their Scottish home. Both are vital to Tanqueray Ten – the citrus heart of the spirit is first distilled in Tiny Tim using fresh chopped oranges, limes and grapefruit, and this is then transferred to the larger, hand-riveted Old Tom, where juniper (more than in the standard version), coriander, angelica, liquorice, camomile flowers and more limes are added.

In order to preserve the vibrant citrus character, only 60% of the final run is selected to go forward for reduction and eventual bottling. Unusually, Tanqueray is made using the one-shot process, another nod to tradition and further evidence of the carefully crafted nature of this superb creation. Finally, I'm glad to say that it's reassuringly strong (something to remember when comparing prices). At 47.3% this offers body, mouthfeel and a delightfully mouth-coating creaminess; this is a classic that continues to deliver from aroma to finish.

Indeed, I'd go so far as to say that you might never need to try another gin ever again. But in doing that you would deny yourself the considerable pleasure of Tanqueray's most recent limited-edition releases Rangpur and Flor de Sevilla, which, though they were only produced for a short run, can still be found on some bar and specialist shelves. Of course, 'limited edition' is a relative term: most craft distillers would be thrilled to sell in a year the 10,000 cases that typically constitute a Tanqueray special release. Perhaps, if sufficiently well received, they'll be kept on.

I don't usually do marks, but I have to give Ten 10/10!

92

TARQUIN'S

BRAND OWNER: Southwestern Distillery Ltd

DISTILLERY: Southwestern Distillery, St Ervan,
Wadebridge, Cornwall

WEBSITE: www.southwesterndistillery.com

VISITOR CENTRE: No

STRENGTH: 42%

OTHER VARIANTS: Seadog Navy Strength

This makes quite the contrast with Tanqueray – not least on scale. Here we are with Tarquin Leadbetter of the eponymous Tarquin's gin in Cornwall, which one could describe as bold, experimental, innovative and quite funky. All the things a small craft distiller is supposed to be in fact, though recent Tanqueray releases show that the message is getting through to the big boys, who are definitely raising their game under pressure from the craft distillers – David to their Goliath perhaps.

I was interested to read Tarquin's blog for 24 January 2013 when he had just really got started. He began: 'It has been 220,240 hours since my last paid employment (in a bar), and over 400,000 hours since I last worked behind a desk. In this period, I had over 4,988 sips of gin and pastis, tasting about 100 different brands. I sent and received 8,132 emails, drove 11,001 miles (had one puncture) and grew a beard for 90.6 days, a personal record.'

It might be worth re-reading that if you are thinking of starting your own distillery. In fact, you might want to print it out and stick it where you (and your partner) can gaze thoughtfully upon it on a regular basis. Without labouring the point, starting your own business – any business – is seriously hard work and, fun though it may seem, starting a distillery is no different. (Writing, on the other hand, is a breeze. The world definitely needs more writers, and drinks books in particular are in short supply. Note use of irony here.)

Tarquin's is batch distilled in a direct-fired copper pot still (a very similar set-up to that at 58 Gin) and, using the one-shot method, he is able to produce a maximum of 300 bottles at once. Interestingly, Tanqueray also adopts this approach, though they make rather more. Their distiller doesn't then bottle and wax-seal each bottle.

He has picked some unusual but not completely outrageous botanicals, including fresh citrus fruits, cacao, pink peppercorns and violet leaves. With great local support, Tarquin's has now reached the point where it has been able to install a second still and now even employs its own brand ambassadors. It just proves what can be done – but with many more hours, miles and emails.

Good luck to him. Anyone who can also distil the UK's first aniseed spirit and call it Cornish Pastis deserves to succeed!

93

THREE RIVERS

BRAND OWNER: Central Line Holdings Ltd

DISTILLERY: City of Manchester Distillery,
21 Red Bank Parade, Manchester

WEBSITE: www.manchesterthreerivers.com

VISITOR CENTRE: Yes

STRENGTH: 40%

OTHER VARIANTS: None

What does it tell us about Manchester, or indeed gin, that one of the most highly rated attractions on TripAdvisor in all of this fine city is the £95 Gin Experience to be had at the brand spanking new (it only opened its doors in 2016) City of Manchester distillery?

Remarkably, 99% of the reviewers (more than 170 of them as we go to press) rated it Excellent or Very Good. There were only two Very Good ratings (one wonders what on earth went wrong) so let's conclude from the wisdom of crowds that the City of Manchester is getting something very right indeed.

It's certainly a professional outfit, with a well-organised website and some serious investment evident in the smart bar and visitor facilities; shiny Arnold Holstein still and an impressive line-up of mini stills where visitors can make their own bottle of gin after choosing from the more than fifty botanicals on offer. They're not alone in offering this type of interactive experience which, as well as providing a very useful revenue stream, sends a stream of eager but unpaid brand ambassadors out to spread the word. It's very good marketing and a jolly good time appears to be had by all.

There's nothing outrageous or deliberately provocative about the product itself. Not to damn with faint praise, but this is fairly mainstream – and all the better for that – but enlivened by the addition of oats to an otherwise conventional enough make-up of botanicals, though cardamom and black pepper make their presence felt alongside the regulation juniper. It's smooth, creamy and warming. A suggested serve features a garnish of fresh cherries which is unusual but brings some pleasantly fruity notes to the fore.

The presence of those intriguing oats is a nod to the history of the nearby Angel Meadow. Apparently, the area was anything but angelic, and the impoverished inhabitants got by on thin rations. Dr Johnson famously defined oats as 'a grain, which in England is generally given to horses, but in Scotland supports the people'. That was in 1755; evidently life was little improved by the Victorian age for the anonymous masses more or less enslaved in the factories of the Industrial Revolution. They famously took some solace in gin. Well, things have clearly moved on and for the better.

The 'three rivers', in case you were wondering, are the Irwell, Irk and Medlock. I never knew that.

94

TIPTREE GIN LIQUEURS

BRAND OWNER:	Wilkin & Sons
DISTILLERY:	Hayman Distillers, Witham, Essex
WEBSITE:	www.tiptree.com
VISITOR CENTRE:	Yes
STRENGTH:	28%
OTHER VARIANTS:	Raspberry, Damson, Rhubarb

Combine two family-owned and fiercely independent companies and products as archetypally English as gin and strawberry jam and what do you get? Simply scrumptious and totally yummy strawberry gin liqueur, that's what. A taste of summer in a bottle of gin – what's not to like?

Long-established preserves maker Wilkin & Sons of Tiptree fame have teamed up with their neighbours at Hayman's who operate just a few miles down the road to create a sensational range of gin fruit liqueurs – English Strawberry, Raspberry, Damson, and Rhubarb using fruit all grown on the Tiptree Farm infused in Hayman's classic London Dry gin (see entry 46).

I suppose that if you are a died-in-the-wool, hard-core gin traditionalist you might object that these are not gins, but then they don't claim to be: 'Gin Liqueur' is quite prominent on the label, which is modelled on the comfortably familiar Tiptree preserves label. What's more, the product is bottled at a respectably strong 28% and, after the first glorious hit of fruit, traditional gin notes are quite apparent.

Both the English Strawberry and Raspberry varieties smell and taste exactly like their namesakes and will appeal if you have a sweet tooth; the Damson is drier and agreeably bitter; and the Rhubarb probably the subtlest of the four. If you like full-strength rhubarb gins, there are now several to choose from. Not one of them a gooseberry.

The range was launched in late 2015 and the first batch sold out almost immediately. The original release featured Tiptree's Little Scarlet Strawberry (a tiny wild variety that is hand-picked at the farm) but that would appear to have been largely supplanted by a generic strawberry version. The Little Scarlet, very much a Tiptree flagship, remains available in a Cocktail Set but that comes with jam jar 'cocktail glasses' which may be just a trifle hipster for many of us.

That apart, these are really delicious products and great fun for summer cocktails. You can drink them neat (all too easily) but I'd suggest mixing with some chilled prosecco to create your own version of a Gin Royale. Alternatively, serve with a good tonic and an appropriate fruit garnish for a memorable and stylish afternoon picnic – if you can't get tickets to Wimbledon, then the essence of Wimbledon can come to your back garden, without all the queuing and inevitable disappointment as the last British player goes out!

95

TWO BIRDS

BRAND OWNER: Union Distillers Ltd

DISTILLERY: Union Distillery, Market Harborough, Leicestershire

WEBSITE: www.twobirdsspirits.co.uk

VISITOR CENTRE: Yes

STRENGTH: 40%

OTHER VARIANTS: Cocktail Strength (trade only), Sipping Gin, Hogarth's Old Tom

Right out of its nest, Two Birds was awarded Gold Medal (UK Craft Gin of the Year) at the Craft Gin Awards 2013. Not bad for this fledgling firm of distillers, based in Market Harborough and producing their spirits on a still of their own design.

Co-owner Mark Gamble is himself an electrical engineer, so he designed and built their twenty-five-litre copper and brass still himself, nicknaming it 'Gerard's No. 1'. I have no idea who Gerard might be, and while it's more usual to give a gin still a lady's name, there's no law against making it masculine if that's what takes your fancy. By the way, this really and truly is a small-batch operation: Gerard can only make around one hundred bottles per four-hour distillation run, so volumes are always going to be very limited.

The botanicals in Two Birds are really held to the minimum; there being a mere five components. What they are remains a strict trade secret, but apart from the key ingredient of juniper (it's fairly obvious the moment you nose this) and what I suspect is orris root (for smoothness and to integrate the gin), I believe there is a citrus element playing its part. What this does show is that it's perfectly possible, indeed you might argue even desirable, to make a perfectly decent gin in the classic London Dry style without complicating matters with a very long list of increasingly arcane ingredients.

However, if the product is simple in its construction don't be fooled. This will stand comparison with any number of the bigger brands and represents a very drinkable, mainstream gin that will work well in a G&T and a range of cocktails. For the drinks trade Two Birds have cleverly devised a more assertive juniper-influenced version, Cocktail Gin – the name should let you work out what it's designed to do.

Alongside the straightforward recipe goes straightforward but nonetheless charming packaging. It's reminiscent of our old friend the Oslo bottle. Hard to tell at a glance but the bolder shoulders give the game away and the bottle has been dressed in some chirpy yet distinctive hand-drawn graphics that reflect this gin's 'countryside spirit'.

I'd love to see this at a higher strength, say 46% abv, which I feel would add just a little bit of punch and weight to what is a very agreeable, well-made and straightforward gin and let those Two Birds soar even higher! But perhaps that's over-egging it (sorry, didn't even try to resist that).

96

UNGAVA

BRAND OWNER: Domaine Pinnacle Inc.,
Frelighsburg, Quebec, Canada

DISTILLERY: Domaine Pinnacle, Cowansville,
Quebec, Canada

WEBSITE: www.ungava-gin.com

VISITOR CENTRE: Boutique available to visit
(though primarily for cider)

STRENGTH: 43.1%

OTHER VARIANTS: None

We haven't had a gin from Canada yet, so this piqued my curiosity. The name and packaging are funky and the colour draws the eye. Ah yes, that colour. When the company's president told Canada's *MacLean's Magazine* that it was 'a bit like morning's vitamin-enriched urine', there's not a lot more to say. Let's move on.

Ungava comes from Quebec and contains some seriously obscure botanicals in an effort to create a gin that is truly, pre-colonially Canadian. So, some forty indigenous herbs, berries and flowers (anything planted by Europeans was out) finally gave way to just six ingredients, all found on the Ungava Peninsula in Nunavik. Cloudberries, crowberries, Labrador tea, Ukiurtatuq or 'Arctic blend' (basically another plant used by native people to make tea), and of course juniper, without which Ungava wouldn't be proper gin (ha, so they do pay some attention to us Europeans, after all). And the crazy colour: that comes from the sixth ingredient, wild rosehips.

The company themselves get pretty lyrical about Ungava, a vast and wild territory at the northern edge of Quebec. Its Inuit meaning is 'towards the open water' and it's described as 'a place of indescribable beauty whose splendour is heightened by the celestial light show of the aurora borealis and the immensity of its landscapes' et cetera et cetera. Their publicity goes on in this vein at some length – not so indescribable after all, it turns out. But, as I haven't been there and won't be going any time soon, we'll take their word for it.

Once a year, two hardy Inuit chaps from Kuujjuaq head out to pick the botanicals. They've got just four weeks to harvest several hundred kilos which are then sent about 900 miles south to a micro-distillery in Cowansville, about an hour's drive from Montreal. A neutral spirit made with locally grown corn is infused with the botanicals. From start to finish, it takes about a month to make a batch of gin, which comes out of the distillery at 72% alcohol and then gets diluted to 43.1% for bottling. Along the way, the Nunavik botanicals are added at the beginning of the process, and again towards the end.

Maintaining the Inuit connection, the funny squiggles on the label aren't some meaningless jumble of lines, but Inuktitut. I haven't the slightest idea what it means. Sorry.

97

VICTORY

BRAND OWNER: Max and Máire Chater

DISTILLERY: Victory Distillery, Tower Bridge, London

WEBSITE: www.victorylondon.co.uk

VISITOR CENTRE: Try the Bump Caves cocktail bar in Tower Bridge

STRENGTH: 43.3%

OTHER VARIANTS: None

Victory Gin appears in George Orwell's most famous novel, *1984*. It's not a cheery read and nor was it intended to be. And the spirit itself, emblematic of the 'creaking camaraderie oiled by gin' that characterises Oceania, is described in unappetising terms: oily-tasting and swallowed to block out the drab realities of life rather than for pleasure. Orwell is harking back to the gins of eighteenth-century London that fuelled the addiction of a semi-comatose population; gin here is the mechanism by which the people are controlled and neutralised as a political force. At the book's harrowing conclusion the protagonist Winston, now a virtual alcoholic, is weeping 'gin-scented tears' as he comes to accept his love for Big Brother.

An odd choice of name, then. Fortunately, today's Victory Gin is a very different product. Gin in *1984* sounds like the cheapest of badly made compound gins, flavoured with cloves for the patrons of the Chestnut Tree Café – this, thankfully, is very different. First of all, there are no cloves in here; rather, this is a proper, juniper-led gin made in small batches by husband and wife team, Max and Máire Chater.

Production is by means of a rotary evaporator, permitting distillation at significantly lower temperatures than a conventional still, thus preserving the delicacy of the botanicals, as well as being more energy-efficient. Victory are not the only small producer using this technology but they are unusual in redistilling their spent botanicals in water to extract aromatics lost in the initial stage. This is truly a hand-crafted product, so availability will be limited even if plans to increase production come to pass.

The concern for sustainability isn't confined to the distilling process: you can play your part by buying Victory in eco-pouches. Save money, save the planet and, as they say, 'be everyone's favourite person at the next party you go to!' The pouches, as you've probably guessed, are similar to 'bag in box' wine containers and simply require you to refill the somewhat utilitarian bottle when it's empty, rather than throwing it in the rubbish and buying another one. It works very well for busy bars (there's a 2.1-litre version) and reduces waste packaging by more than 80%.

Classically juniper-forward, there is one unusual botanical here in chestnut – a nod to Orwell's café perhaps? And look for the Morse code 'V' on the label. Victory is subtler than it first appears.

WARNER EDWARDS
HARRINGTON DRY

BRAND OWNER:	Warner Edwards Distillery Ltd
DISTILLERY:	Warner Edwards, Falls Farm, Harrington, Northants
WEBSITE:	www.warneredwards.com
VISITOR CENTRE:	Yes
STRENGTH:	44%
OTHER VARIANTS:	Elderflower, Sloe, Rhubarb, Botanical Garden

I hesitate to refer to anyone as 'passionate' about their product. The problem with this perfectly good, inoffensive and hitherto useful word is that it has been entirely devalued by the marketing community (PR folks are particularly egregious offenders). 'Passion' is everywhere, and as a result it's nowhere – empty of all meaning, an empty cliché that has been hollowed out and now lies dully on the page, gasping for its last breath like a stranded dolphin.

Unfortunately, I can't think of another word to describe Tom Warner's enthusiasm for his product. Talking to him, it was hard to get a word in edgeways; such was the tumbling rush of ardent advocacy that I was quite caught up in his zeal. Here, I felt, was a man alive with a mission to share, to explain, to proselytise about his product, so intensely felt that I may as well have been in the presence of the Ancient Mariner – not the gin of the same name but the bloke in the poem – and I could not choose but hear.

And what a great story he tells Warner Edwards Harrington Dry has been created by two chums from agricultural college (Tom and business partner Sion Edwards) looking for an escape from a life of corporate conformity by embracing the vicissitudes of self-employment; something, incidentally, which I can entirely empathise with, having long since fallen foul of dull convention. And several employers.

Springing as they both do from long-established farming stock, they looked at first at distilling essential oils from lavender they planned to grow on the family farms. They briefly toyed with making vodka but, thankfully, then remembered they liked gin. Hallelujah!

Being committed to the idea, they bought one of the first small Holstein stills in the UK and fired it up in December 2012 (that's a measure of just how new this craft gin phenomenon is) and have gone from strength to strength.

And so they should. This is a bold and proudly assertive, juniper-led, peppery and complex product that should appeal to traditionalists looking to push the boundaries of flavour just a little, without anything too outrageous or provocatively unconventional. Use in cocktails where you want the gin to shine through and for best results in a G&T (don't overdo the tonic). Judges at the San Francisco World Spirits Competition thought highly enough of this to award it Double Gold – one each for Tom and Sion, presumably, united in spirit.

99

WHITLEY NEILL

BRAND OWNER: Halewood International
Holdings plc

DISTILLERY: The Langley Distillery, Langley
Green, Warley, West Midlands

WEBSITE: www.whitleyneill.com

VISITOR CENTRE: No

STRENGTH: 43%

OTHER VARIANTS: Blood Orange, Raspberry,
Rhubarb & Ginger, Quince

Drat! More of that pesky dark glass that doesn't allow you to see how much is left in the bottle. Aren't those bottles annoying? Gin is a wonderfully clear and bright spirit, so why hide it away?[1] Anyway, enough of that: we're approaching the end of this wonderful gin odyssey and that's reason enough to be cheerful.

What we have here is another gin inspired by Africa (I trust you've remembered the elephants and our trip to trendy Tooting) but brought to us by Johnny Neill, fourth-generation member of the Greenall Whitley distilling dynasty. He's got gin in his blood and, as it happens, a South African wife. Taking that as his cue, he turned to the physalis plant and the baobab tree – known as the 'tree of life' – to add the flavour of the Dark Continent to this most English of spirits. The latter's strange, otherworldly, upside-down form features as the brand's logo.

Launched in 2007, Whitley Neill was an early entrant into the small-batch gin scene and has since picked up a hatful of medals for its complex, spicy taste with the layered earth notes, hints of tropical fruits and lemons and peppery finish. Much play is made on their website of the copper pot still (Constance, since you asked) used to make the gin, and which is said to be England's oldest. I don't actually think this matters, though you may feel it adds a certain corroborative and romantic detail to the story.

At first Whitley Neill offered only one product, but in the first edition of this book I offered the thought that 'it will be interesting to see how this approach serves the brand'. Well, they've subsequently gone down the road of flavoured variants with some enthusiasm, offering a whole fruit basket of different expressions (see opposite and check their website for the most recent), offering an overflowing cornucopia of zesty gin goodness.

I think that's probably about it. Time that you put this down and picked up a refreshing G&T, White Lady, Negroni, Old Etonian or Martini. I told you that gin was simply The Last Word. And, with that, I'm off for a handy Corpse Reviver No. 2. Pip! Pip!

No. Wait. There's yet more. And trust me, they are both rip-snortingly good. Yes, as good as that, whatever it means.

....

[1] Actually one reason is that it keeps better. I just drink it faster though; that works as well.

100

WHITTAKER'S ORIGINAL

BRAND OWNER: Harrogate Distillery Ltd

DISTILLERY: Whittaker's Gin, Harewell House Farm, Dacre Banks, Harrogate, N. Yorkshire

WEBSITE: www.whittakersgin.com

VISITOR CENTRE: Yes

STRENGTH: 42%

OTHER VARIANTS: Navy Strength, Pink Particular, Clearly Sloe

There are lots of awards out there for various spirits. It's something of a growth industry as shrewd publishers and various entrepreneurially-minded folk note that distillers like to have little gold and silver stickers to affix to their bottles and so launch their awards to compete with the more established (and, dare I say, widely recognised) schemes. Still, one sticker looks much like another when viewed on an off-licence shelf and so the proliferation of awards continues. As a buccaneering Scotch whisky distiller of my acquaintance once observed, the industry 'chases more worthless medals than an African despot'. Not very PC but brutally candid.

The point, of course, is that not all awards are equal. But if awards keep piling up it's worth taking a good look at the recipient. Whittaker's – a relative newcomer – have been entering competitions since 2015 and have aced a good few, including awards from the IWSC and ISC; the Craft Distilling Expo and the American Distilling Institute. Now, those latter names might not mean much to you but they're indicative of Whittaker's being recognised by and arguably rising above their peers. Especially in the USA, where there is a very large craft distilling scene, this represents praise indeed.

Little wonder, then, that this farm-based distillery from near Harrogate has rapidly expanded from one small 100-litre Hill Billy Stills' import from Bourbon Country in Kentucky to four units manufactured in nearby Tadcaster, increasing their distilling capacity more than a dozen times greater.

The range has expanded too, to include the Original, a Navy Strength, a Sloe variant and the charmingly named Pink Particular (pink peppercorns, pink hibiscus and cardamom are the signature botanicals at work here). Shrewdly, they make it easy for us to try all the products, offering them in small (20cl), medium (50cl) and large (70cl) bottles – something that other small brands might like to copy.

Reflecting its Yorkshire antecedents, this is not a gin that's shy and bashful! Lots of earthy juniper will grab your attention but there are hints of the lemon groves in there and drying spices to give the palate plenty to hang on to. Classy stuff.

Finally, a word on the handsome labels. With a base at Harewell House Farm, the hare was a logical and emotional choice to grace the packaging and very fine it looks, too.

101

XORIGUER

BRAND OWNER:	M Pons Justo SA
DISTILLERY:	Destilerias Xoriguer, Mahón, Menorca
WEBSITE:	www.xoriguer.co.uk
VISITOR CENTRE:	No
STRENGTH:	38%
OTHER VARIANTS:	None

$\mathcal{H}aving$ begun with a numeral and then gone straight into the letter A, I determined to finish this with a Z. There is a Zebra gin apparently, distilled by the splendidly named Four Stars Beverages Ltd of 183/189 Bombo Road Kawempe-Kazo, Kampala, in Uganda. But my joy was short-lived. Could I find a bottle? What do you think? Those stripes are better camouflage than you first realise.

Tragically, the makers of the intriguingly named Zymurgorium Marmalade Gin never responded to my increasingly desperate entreaties for information. They'll be sorry now!

Thus we conclude with Xoriguer from the Spanish Balearic island of Menorca and which turns out to have the most fascinating story imaginable. For one thing, there are only two gins left in the world enjoying recognition as a local speciality. And there's a connection to the Jolly Jack Tars of Britain's Royal Navy. In the eighteenth century Menorca was British and we had a huge base there. And, in the middle of the Gin Craze, what do you imagine thirsty British matelots wanted to drink? Hint: the answer is not 'rum'. So, the locals made gin for them and today they're still at it.

And, unusually, it is distilled using a base of Mediterranean wine alcohol but comes off the wood-fired stills at its 38% bottling strength. It comes in a seriously funky bottle with a label that is genuinely retro (largely because no one has got round to changing it in years). What's not to like?

It gets better. It is, of course, still family-owned and distilled to a secret recipe. Apparently only heirs of the founder Miguel Pons Justo are permitted to receive the super classified details and proportions of the vital ingredients, and before they add them to the still the doors are locked and any witnesses killed. Actually I made that last bit up – they just politely ask them to leave. But say you did believe me, if only for a moment.

Before bottling, it is rested in oak. You can find a bottle here in the UK for around £23. I can't tell you how happy it has made me to track down Xoriguer (say it 'sho-ri-gair') – a truly artisanal gin, with deep and long-standing connections to the great days of English gin distilling that is still alive and flourishing as we enter a new gin craze.

Bottoms up, ladies and gentlemen!

102

A SHORT HISTORY OF TONIC WATER

❋

I'm often asked what tonic water I prefer. Once upon a time, that would have been easy: there was Schweppes and the other, cheaper ones. So, Schweppes it was – but here's a short history.

You owe two nineteenth-century French scientists a big drink. Back in 1820, Pierre-Joseph Pelletier and Joseph Caventou worked out how to extract quinine from the bark of the cinchona tree, which grows in the foothills of the Andes. Aware of its wonderful properties in treating malaria, the local natives called it the 'fever tree'. In fact, bark had been shipped to Europe for centuries, though, aware of its value, the newly independent republics of Peru, Ecuador, Colombia and Bolivia strictly controlled the export of seeds and seedlings.

But, with their empires expanding fast into tropical regions, the French and British were desperate to produce larger quantities and control the supply. In 1865 Charles Ledger succeeded in smuggling seeds out of Bolivia which were eventually successfully cultivated in the Dutch colony of Java. The species he pilfered, rich in quinine, was cultivated and renamed *Cinchona ledgeriana* and went on to dominate the world supply of quinine.

However, though effective in preventing malaria and other tropical fevers, quinine is horribly bitter to the taste. Dissolved in the carbonated water pioneered by one Johann Jacob Schweppe it became a more palatable tonic – and with the addition of gin was enthusiastically adopted by the British in India. Hurrah!

Returning colonials brought the fashion for gin and tonic back home and added some respectability to gin's raffish image. A classic was born.

Sadly, though, over the years, the amount of quinine was reduced and, for cost reasons, artificial sweeteners were employed. Tonic water slowly followed gin into a dark place, but in recent years this has all changed.

As a well-known brand maintains: 'If three quarters of your gin and tonic is the tonic, make sure you use the best.' Fever-Tree was born on the back of the boom in premium crafted gins and today has spawned many imitators such as 1724, Merchant's Heart, Bermondsey, East Imperial, Fentimans, Walter Gregor's, Lamb & Watt, Thomas Henry, BTW and so on.

But one brand that I've been trying recently and enjoyed comes, surprisingly, from good old Britvic, though they don't shout about that. The London Essence Company is a revival of a business founded in 1896 to produce essential oils and essences. Their collection of tonic waters and ginger ale was created in collaboration with the renowned cocktail guru Nick Strangeway. Using distilled essences, the flavours are subtle but delicious and low in sugar.

You can get cheaper tonics – but is that really what you want?

ACKNOWLEDGEMENTS

Thanks are due to all the distillers, too many to mention by name, who let me look around their distilleries and patiently answered my tedious and no doubt naïve questions. My long-suffering wife Lindsay put up with the vicissitudes of my moods while writing this book (but I suspect the sampling helped); my agent Judy Moir skilfully guided me through the arcane rituals of actually getting a publisher interested; and the team at said publisher, Birlinn – especially Neville Moir, Alison Rae, Anna Marshall, Laura Poynton and Jan Rutherford (dedicated gin drinkers all) – were committed and enthusiastic supporters.

The gin industry generously stepped up with samples and to all the 101 listed here and to the others who responded but I have disappointed, my thanks. And, to the few who spurned my entreaties, I trust you're feeling good about that right now. Special thanks to Alex Nicol (Spencerfield Spirits); Master of Malt's Ben Ellefsen and his colleagues who helped get this off the ground; and especially to designer Teresa Monachino for her fine work.

All trademarks are acknowledged, and all product images are the copyright property of the relevant brand owner, reproduced with permission.